# LOST PROVINCE

## ALSO BY STEPHEN HENIGHAN

*Other Americas* (novel)
*Nights in the Yungas* (short stories)
*The Places Where Names Vanish* (novel)
*North of Tourism* (short stories)
*Assuming the Light: The Parisian Literary Apprenticeship
of Miguel Angel Asturias* (criticism)
*When Words Deny the World: The Reshaping of Canadian Writing* (essays)

# LOST PROVINCE
Adventures in a Moldovan Family

## STEPHEN HENIGHAN

an imprint of Beach Holme Publishing
PROSPECT BOOKS
VANCOUVER, BC

This book is published by Beach Holme Publishing, 226–2040 West 12th Avenue, Vancouver, B.C. V6J 2G2. *www.beachholme.bc.ca*. This is a Prospect Book.

The publisher gratefully acknowledges the financial support of the Canada Council for the Arts and of the British Columbia Arts Council. The publisher also acknowledges the financial assistance received from the Government of Canada through the Book Publishing Industry Development Program (BPIDP) for its publishing activities.

The Canada Council | Le Conseil des Arts
for the Arts | du Canada

BRITISH
COLUMBIA
ARTS COUNCIL
Supported by the Province of British Columbia

Editor: Michael Carroll
Design and Production: Jen Hamilton
Cover Art: © Paul Schutzer/ALPHA-PRESSE
Author Photograph: Martin Schwalbe

Printed and bound in Canada by Kromar Printing Ltd.

**National Library of Canada Cataloguing in Publication Data**

Henighan, Stephen, 1960-
  Lost province: adventures in a Moldovan family/Stephen Henighan.

"A prospect book."
ISBN 0-88878-432-5

1. Henighan, Stephen, 1960- —Journeys—Moldova. 2. Moldova—Social life and customs. 3. Moldova—Description and travel.
4. Moldova—Languages. 5. Moldavian dialect. 6. English teachers—Moldova—Biography. I. Title.
DK509.29.H46 2002      947.608'6      C2002-911088-2

# CONTENTS

# 1

# JOURNEY INTO DIFFERENCE

In early 1989, a few months after the election that sealed the Canada-U.S. Free Trade Agreement and a few months before the fall of the Berlin Wall, I made a long trip through Hungary, Czechoslovakia, and Poland. The prospect of free trade depressed me. I brooded about the survival of the peculiarities of habit, language, architecture, outlook, and attitude, nurtured by local and national cultures, which furnished the world with much of the multiplicity and fascination that made living worthwhile. In Central Europe I thought I glimpsed the revival of the thriving diversity of *Mitteleuropa*—the return of an older, more complicated Europe. Time would prove this resuscitation of heterodoxy to be a mirage, but in 1989 I felt I had received a great gift, stumbling upon a treasure trove of multiplicity in an era when differences were being irreducibly flattened. I promised myself I would return to the far side of Europe.

I went back to Canada and lived for two and a half years in Montreal, writing fiction and journalism and supporting myself with odd jobs. When, in 1992, I decided to give up my freelancer's life to write a doctoral thesis at the University of Oxford, part of my motivation for studying in England stemmed from a longing to be close to the Europe that had intrigued me. On gloomy Oxford days I dreamed of escaping to *Mitteleuropa*. My next journey east, though, was not to be to the former realm of the Austro-Hungarian Empire, but to the Balkans.

In 1989 I had not visited the Balkans: my knowledge of the region derived from literature. One image that made a strong impression on me, having travelled through Hungary, Czechoslovakia, and Poland with Olivia Manning's *The Balkan Trilogy* in my backpack, was the annexation of Bessarabia. Essentially a portrait of a marriage, Manning's novels are set against the background of Romania's entry into World War II. Stalin's annexation of Bessarabia in 1940, though it takes place offstage, contributes powerfully to the suffocation of hope that eventually drives the central characters to flee Bucharest. The Romanian characters, of course, stay behind in Romania. Bessarabians, too, stayed behind—no longer citizens of Romania, but of the Soviet Union.

The image had dimmed by the time I applied for a summer teaching job in Romania in 1994. A year and a half earlier, during a period of boredom with my doctoral thesis, I had started studying Romanian. After taking four hours of introductory lessons with a postdoctoral student who knew the language well, I invested in a grammar book, discovered a cache of tapes, and happily devoted my idle hours to memorizing the unpredictable plural forms of Romanian nouns. By the summer I was aching to practise the language. I had spent the year as president of my Oxford college's graduate-student association—a wearing responsibility that had added thirty or more hours of commitments every week to my already-packed schedule, binding me to the mandates of a community both demanding and insular. A lingering romantic confusion had pulled the narrow borders of this world a notch tighter. I needed to get away.

Little did I suspect how far away I was going.

Three weeks before I was due to leave for Romania I received a letter informing me that I had been transferred to Chişinău in the

Republic of Moldova, in the former Soviet Union. Here, too, the letter assured me, I would be able to speak Romanian. A phone call established that my sponsor organization had been expelled from Romania (rumour claimed its employees had been caught forging Romanian work permits). I did some research, discovered Moldova was Bessarabia, called back, and said I would agree to the transfer on the condition that I was lodged with a Romanian, rather than a Russian-speaking, family. I was told this would be arranged. The voice on the phone mentioned that I would be travelling from London overland to Chişinău (pronounced *Kee-she-now*). They knew I would enjoy the trip.

I boarded the yellow London-Lvov Liner (the name was painted on the bus's side) at Victoria Station. The passengers were divided between young volunteers travelling to Ukraine, Belarus, and Moldova, and elderly British Ukrainians returning to visit relatives. The English teachers' bulging luggage blocked the ventilation system, and everyone sweated. We crossed the English Channel at midnight and awoke in the morning on a highway that insulated us from difference. Belgium slipped into Holland and then into Germany with scarcely a wrinkle of recognition. Only in eastern Germany did evidence of a transition appear: stretches of older, rougher highway, drab stucco farmhouses, the occasional Skoda or Lada tagging behind faster-moving traffic. At the Polish border the immigration post was flying the blue-and-gold European Union flag optimistically alongside the red-and-white of Poland. Viewed from the highway, Poland appeared emptier than I remembered: the forests dark, the fields untended. Jazzy roadside gas bars erupted in the mid-distance, their restaurants equalling any installation along a U.S. interstate for utter featurelessness. Only the possibility of ordering sausages and pierogies, in addition to hamburgers, french fries, and Cokes, offered a reminder that this was not Kansas. The British teachers, not having encountered Polish food before, looked on with discomfort moderating into fascination as I savoured a culinary favourite I remembered from my Canadian childhood, slurping up a plate of delicious pierogies swimming in spiced cream. Gazing into my colleagues' disconsolate faces (their french fries were stale), I thought: *Another testament to the advantages of multicultural societies!*

Multiculturalism, which often boiled down to the doomed exercise of trying to preserve a culture in the absence of the language in which the culture was inscribed, presented both an example and a warning. Riding the bus over the Polish plains, I listened on my Walkman to a trans-European rock music station whose disc jockeys spoke blaring U.S. English: "Whether you're in St. Petersburg, Russia, or Venice, Italy, we mean *rock!*" Voices would call in from Athens or Dresden or Zagreb or Madrid and request rock songs in accented English. In this context national European cultures commanded no more authority or integrity than the culture of a Portuguese community in Toronto or an Italian neighbourhood in Montreal. Critics of Canadian multiculturalism argued that it trivialized cultures, shrinking them to picturesque folklore; the same danger, on a vastly larger scale, underlay cultural globalization. All of Italy risked becoming little more than the "Italian neighbourhood" of a culturally homogenized planet incapable of expressing or sanctioning assumptions, attitudes, or emotional, spiritual, or cultural allegiances not comfortably contained within the forms of the rock video or the talk-show confession. The day when all of the world's business and entertainment would take place in English, demoting national languages and cultures to the property of peasant grandmothers and the poorly educated, did not seem far off as, rumbling through the Polish night, I listened to an American DJ in Amsterdam shout across Europe: "Heinrich in Vienna is just dying to hear Tina Turner!"

I was travelling east in search of differences that had endured. I was destined to be disillusioned and enlightened in a variety of ways. I was looking forward to discovering in Moldova a plucky little republic, wedged between Ukraine and Romania, valiantly recovering its cultural specificity after more than fifty years of Soviet occupation.

But this was not what I found.

The first warning shot across my bow struck at the Polish-Ukrainian border. The disintegration of the Soviet Union, supposedly dead and buried three years earlier, was proceeding at roughly the pace at which rust creeps into metal. Border formalities to enter Ukraine consumed three and a half hours. (Having spent two consecutive nights on the Liner, most of us responded badly to this harassment.) Immigration procedures were hamstrung by archaic forms and formalities. We were handed scrappy grey pieces of paper to fill in; all spoke not of Ukraine, but of the Soviet Union. A record of every dollar, deutschmark, złoty, or pound we were carrying had to be crammed into narrow spaces in small, striped boxes. The justification for completing these forms had disappeared: Ukraine was officially a market economy, free of currency controls and the mandatory daily exchanges that had characterized the old Eastern Europe. Yet Soviet norms continued to be enforced. We even had to sign an absurd pledge to present for inspection to the authorities of the Soviet Union all "printed matter, manuscripts, films, sound recordings, postage stamps, graphics, etc."

Then we were herded single-file from one end of a cavernous room to the other. Our declarations were examined and our transit visas stamped. As we were about to return to the Liner, the officer in charge announced he wanted to "verify our declarations." He would search every passenger, counting the money each of us was carrying to check that it corresponded to our declarations.

The passengers groaned, too exhausted to retaliate. Our team of three drivers went berserk. They began screaming at the officer, waving their arms and backing him into a corner until guards stepped up on either side to protect him. The drivers, all the while, were surreptitiously motioning us onto the Liner. We took the hint and fled. By the time the drivers had completed their harangue, every passenger was seated. The drivers scrambled onboard, gunned the engine, and pulled away from the border post. A customs official stepped out onto the blacktop and shouted at the driver. But it was too late: we had fled.

Soviet forms and procedures remained in force, but not Soviet power. We couldn't have made this escape three years earlier.

The transition from Poland to Ukraine was dramatic. We had barely crossed the border when the first silver onion dome soared into sight. The poorly maintained road wound between tiny farmhouses, walled off behind low stone walls. In the yards stood scarved old women, children without shirts or shoes, dust sifting upward around them. The abundant Orthodox churches provided the only glimmer of elegance in this degraded landscape. The fields were smaller and scrubbier than those in Poland, and there were no forests. Half an hour beyond the border a stinking, whitish smog descended, swathing everything in an unhealthy glow that escorted us most of the way to the hideous high-rise blocks on the outskirts of Lvov. Europe's border had advanced since 1989. Poland might not join the European Union for years to come, yet culturally it had leaped over the East European wall.

Unlike Poland, the former Soviet republics retained their cultural eccentricities, their obedience to Soviet bureaucratic norms that Moscow was no longer in a position to enforce, and their poverty. Their cultural reference points consisted of an unlikely conflation of a lingering belief in the centrality of Moscow, and exposure to global mass culture through television; in contrast to the mood in Prague, Budapest, or Warsaw, a yearning to "return to Europe" did not enter the equation. Ukraine, Moldova, and Belarus lay on the wrong side of an imaginary perimeter beyond which Europe did not penetrate.

The trait that distinguished Moldova from the other republics was its historical tie to Romania. Moldova was not Russian and, initially, it had not been part of the Soviet Empire. At various points in its history, most recently from 1944 until 1991, it had been kidnapped. The country was a shard of the Balkans that had been tossed incongruously into the post-Soviet brew. It was prone to Balkan conflicts, such as the brief 1992 war when the fearsome Russian General

Alexander Lebed had thrown the Soviet Fourteenth Army into battle in support of Slavic separatists in the city of Tiraspol, where Russian and Ukrainian speakers formed a majority of the population. Lebed, a former battalion commander in Afghanistan, had put out nationalist brushfires in Armenia and Azerbaijan in 1989 and 1990, but it was in Moldova that he came into his own as a defender of the Russian Empire. In the Fourteenth Army—the massive invasion force groomed by the Soviet Union to overrun Greece and Italy in the event of an all-out war with NATO—Lebed discovered his ideal instrument. As a result of his intervention, an unrecognized Slavic statelet called the Trans-Dniestrian Republic had emerged. Trans-Dniestria's autonomy was guarded by Lebed and his weaponry. No one could be certain where the borders of Moldova ended or began.

But the Republic of Moldova was merely a slice of a larger entity. Moldavia (Moldova in Romanian) was one of the three constituent regions of Romania, the others being Wallachia (Ţara Romanească in Romanian) and Transylvania (Ardeal in Romanian). It was the union of Wallachia and Moldavia in 1859 that had created modern Romania. In 1940 the Molotov-Ribbentrop Pact forced Romania to cede Northern Bukovina, a mountainous region of great cultural richness, to the Soviet Union. Most of Bukovina, including the important city of Cernăuţi, is now inside the borders of Ukraine. Cernăuţi is famous in Romania as the city where Mihai Eminescu, Romania's national poet, was educated in the 1860s; in the 1930s Paul Celan, the great German-Jewish poet, received his education in the same city, where he began his writing career in Romanian before switching to German. Yet the most serious consequence of the Molotov-Ribbentrop Pact was that the eastern half of Moldavia was combined with a thin strip of Ukraine and incorporated into the Soviet Union as the Moldavian Soviet Socialist Republic.

In a sense, it was not Romania that was dismembered by the victors of World War II, but Moldavia. Chişinău, the region's second city, vanished from the Romanian-speaking world. The blow to Romanian identity, which had entered a phase of unprecedented self-confidence during the interwar years, was crippling. With the exception of the witty playwright I. L. Caragiale, a precursor of absurdism and a native of Wallachia, the pillars of late-nineteenth- and early-twentieth-century literature—the country's classics—were all Moldavian: Vasile Alecsandri, the early Romantic poet who was instrumental in developing an indigenous Romanian theatrical tradition; the poet Eminescu; Mihail Sadoveanu, the Balzac-like novelist of gargantuan energy who drenched his dozens of books in the history, language, and teeming natural world of Moldavia; Ion Creangă, the peasant storyteller who mythologized traditional Romanian life. The dismemberment of Moldavia, which had occurred periodically throughout history, seemed this time to have stopped an emerging national tradition in its tracks.

Reading Mircea Eliade's history of Romania as the bus carried me eastward, I learned that Moldavia had reached the zenith of its power under Stephen the Great (1457–1504), one of the most admired monarchs of his day. After Stephen's death, Moldavia fell under Ottoman rule. At the close of the Russo-Turkish War in 1812, Tsar Alexander I sliced Moldavia in half. The area east of the Prut River, renamed Bessarabia, remained under Russian rule. In 1817 the Russians conducted the first census of Bessarabia and discovered that eighty-six percent of the population spoke Romanian, 6.5 percent Ukrainian, and 1.5 percent Russian. By the end of the nineteenth century, after eighty years of forced migrations and assimilationist education policy, only half of Bessarabians spoke Romanian. When Bessarabia was reintegrated into Romania after World War I, Bucharest dispatched Romanian-speaking schoolteachers and administrators to Chişinău to reinforce its claim.

The ebullient if troubled interwar years reconfirmed Bessarabia's Romanian character but also some of its peculiarities. Older people during the 1920s and 1930s retained an attachment to the Cyrillic alphabet, while the upper classes continued to take their cultural cues from Moscow and St. Petersburg. Bucharest's administrators, though often insensitive to local customs, opened new markets to Bessarabian goods and paved roads at a pace that put the Russians to shame. The Romanian schoolteachers raised the literacy rate to thirty percent. In the minds of many intellectuals the two halves of Moldavia, severed for more than a century, had been reunited.

Mihail Sadoveanu expressed this consciousness in historical novels such as *Nunta Dominiție Ruxanda* (*Princess Ruxanda's Wedding*, 1932) set in the seventeenth century when Moldavia, though under Ottoman rule, remained whole. The novel's characters gallop indiscriminately across the length and breadth of Moldavia. The Prut River is stripped of political significance and becomes important primarily as a place to water the horses. At the same time the struggle for cultural wholeness is never far from the centre of the novel's action. Subsequent Soviet propaganda would decry the "primitive" state of the Bessarabians at the time of the 1940 annexation, but during the interwar years a Romanian middle class took root. Bessarabia in 1940 was inextricably entwined in the Romanian national equation. After the 1940 annexation, the Romanian fascist leader General Ion Antonescu fought to recover Bessarabia. In 1941 the Romanian army drove out the Soviet occupying forces. Penetrating deep into the Soviet Union, Antonescu's troops captured the Black Sea port of Odessa. From 1941 to 1944 Bessarabia returned to Romania, plaguing today's Moldovans with the uncomfortable paradox of being one of the few communities in the world that considers itself to have been liberated by a fascist.

In 1944 the Soviet Union reconquered Bessarabia. Vyacheslav Molotov and Joseph Stalin worked far harder than the tsars to alter the territory's character. The respected Romanian dissident Paul Goma, who fled Bessarabia at this time, reports that the Soviet troops burned on large bonfires all books printed in the Latin alphabet. The Red Army staged mass executions of captured Romanian soldiers.

Tests performed on a swamp near the northern Moldovan city of Bălţi have suggested that it may contain the bodies of up to fifty thousand Romanian soldiers. This represents a massacre several times the size of the notorious slaughter of Polish officers by Soviet troops at Katyn in 1943; yet, unlike Katyn, Bălţi has never entered the world's historical consciousness.

During the first year of Soviet occupation, three hundred thousand Romanians were removed from Bessarabia and Northern Bukovina and scattered through Siberia and other remote tracts of the Soviet Union. By 1953 authorities in Moscow had dispatched more than two hundred and fifty thousand Russians, Ukrainians, and Tatars to Bessarabia to serve as civil servants, teachers, soldiers, and police officers. The tally of Romanian-speaking deportees to far-flung districts of the Soviet Union surpassed 1.1 million. The 1946–47 famine killed more than one hundred thousand peasants. The society of "Moldavia beyond the Prut," as Romanians called the region, had been decapitated. Few Romanians endowed with education, initiative, or professional skills were allowed to remain. The Soviet claim of having uplifted a society of peasants maintained in ignorance by the fumbling monarchy in Bucharest was not true in 1940, but within a decade the Romanians of Bessarabia had been reduced to a state nearly as pathetic as that portrayed by Soviet propaganda.

# 2

# THE FAMILY THAT DID NOT KNOW IT SPOKE ROMANIAN

The block letters projecting above the roof of the train station read CHIȘINĂU. At first glance the city had a hard-baked Mediterranean quality. The teachers were marshalled on the platform, our names were read out, and families stepped forward to claim us. I was claimed by Andrei, a dark, stocky twenty-year-old with a military haircut who hustled me toward the taxi stand with a gruff haste I soon realized was born of discomfort. The taxi climbed the hill away from the train station and proceeded down the stately boulevard—lined with imposing early-twentieth-century buildings—that I would come to know as Ștefan Cel Mare (Stephen the Great) Boulevard. Kiosks and crowds thronged the broad sidewalks. We passed parks, a smaller replica of the Arc de Triomphe, people idling in leafy shade. I was dazzled. After ramshackle Lvov, set on its smoggy plain, the Frenchified elegance of some of Chișinău's public buildings, the generosity of the city's layout, and the Latinate street life delighted me. I stared hungrily out the window, eager to get rid of my luggage and dive into this pulse of colour and movement.

I was brought back to reality by the sound of Andrei talking to the taxi driver in Russian. The choice of language surprised me. Andrei, seeming flustered, turned around in the front seat and addressed me with an ungraspable phrase that ended with *"pa russki?"*

I realized he was asking me if I spoke Russian. *"Nu,"* I replied. *"Vorbesc românește."*

The taxi driver looked startled. Andrei tried again. "You don't speak Russian?"

"No, but I speak Romanian."

Andrei and the driver looked at each other, concurring with apparent surprise that I was speaking *Moldavski*. Andrei switched from Russian to a thick, overinflected Romanian. I strained to understand. The taxi climbed a long slope into the district of Buiucani. A row of nine-story high rises stretched along the crest of the hill like a flat-featured palisade. The taxi threaded between two of the high-rise blocks, then trundled over a street running behind the buildings. Across the street lay the bare brown earth of a yard where residents sat on benches beneath sparse shade; barefoot boys in shorts, their torsos burned brown, pelted through the dust. We got out. I removed my luggage, thanking the driver affably in Romanian; in return I received a stony stare. A heavyset woman with a broad, pleasant face got up from one of the benches and walked over to us. She held out her hand.

"Good afternoon," I said in Romanian as we shook hands. "How are you?"

"He speaks *moldoveanu*, Mama," Andrei said in Romanian.

It took me weeks to untangle the linguistic skein into which I had stumbled. At the time of Moldovan independence in 1991, sixty-five percent of the republic's 4.3 million people identified themselves as ethnically Romanian. The remaining thirty-five percent of the population broke down into fourteen percent Ukrainian, thirteen percent Russian, and about eight percent other ethnicities, most notably the Turkic Gagauz people, Bulgarians, and Jews (who were Russian-speaking). These figures, though, were complicated by the dynamics of power. After fifty years of Soviet rule, the language all these groups had in common was Russian; most Romanians spoke Russian, but very few ethnic Russians spoke Romanian. And, as I discovered in the company of my family, many Romanians did not believe they spoke Romanian, either. For fifty years they had been taught to call their language "Moldovan." Soviet doctrine dictated that the language of the Moldavian Soviet Socialist Republic was a backward regional dialect only distantly related to Romanian. Soviet linguists churned out tracts "proving" that the two jurisdictions spoke mutually incomprehensible languages. It is true that the Moldavian version of Romanian has a distinct accent and a more Slavic-influenced lexicon than the Romanian of Bucharest, but to a certain extent these traits are shared by all of historical Moldavia—the part that remained within Romania as well as the present-day Republic of Moldova and Romanian speakers in the portions of the country annexed to Ukraine (where, oddly, Soviet documents continued to refer to the language as Romanian).

Fifty years of Soviet occupation and Russian schooling had made an impact on the vocabulary and accent of the Romanian speakers of Moldova, but their language was instantly recognizable as Romanian—the same Romanian spoken in Romania. It was not even a "dialect" of Romanian (as a recent edition of the Lonely Planet guide *Romania & Moldova* erroneously claims). Professional linguists recognize three dialects of Romanian, which are spoken by Romanian minorities in former Yugoslavia and Albania. But, within the terms of formal linguistics, the language of Romania and the language of Moldova are the same.

The "Moldovan" language was an invention. The notion had been created by Stalin's advisers to erect a mental barricade between the new Soviet republic and Romania. Soviet education policy deepened the gulf by rewriting Romanian in Cyrillic characters. This denied Romanian-speaking graduates of Moldovan schools access to their own literary and historical tradition by keeping most of them in ignorance of the Latin alphabet in which Romanian is written.

Cultural destitution, in turn, strengthened the argument that speakers of "Moldovan" had been ignorant savages until Russian culture was bestowed upon them. Soviet leaders from Joseph Stalin to Mikhail Gorbachev pursued this policy out of a fear of uprisings in favour of reunification with Romania.

The imperative to drum into Moldovans that they spoke a degenerate local patois grew more pressing during the final years of Soviet rule. From the early 1970s onward the maverick Romanian tyrant Nicolae Ceauşescu, his ideological credibility exhausted, relied on nationalism to legitimize his rule. One strain of his ideology, claiming that the richly heterogeneous territory of Transylvania had been Romanian since the beginning of time, inspired the destruction of Transylvanian Hungarian towns and villages, the dispersal of Transylvania's German population, and blatant tampering with archaeological sites that produced evidence incompatible with Ceauşescu's boast that the Romanians were the direct descendants of the Roman Empire and the natural inheritors of its grandeur.

As early as the mid-1960s, Ceauşescu's speeches launched poison darts at the Soviet propaganda version of Moldovan history and identity. Ceauşescu toned down his rhetoric during a period of rapprochement with the Soviets in the 1970s, but by the late 1980s, struggling for his own survival, he played the nationalist card with renewed vigour. Little doubt remains that Gorbachev assisted in Ceauşescu's overthrow in December 1989. Already spooked by other nationalist genies emerging from a variety of bottles and shaken by monstrous demonstrations in Chişinău in 1989 in support of the Latin alphabet and the Romanian flag, Gorbachev was eager to squelch the possibility of rampaging Romanian nationalism on his southwestern flank.

The largely passive recipients of these geopolitical pressures were people like Andrei and his family. They had suffered through the Leonid Brezhnev era when you could be arrested for speaking Romanian on a trolley bus or in a market. They had been told since birth that the language they spoke was called "Moldovan," was written in the Cyrillic alphabet, and was a backward dialect. They had been taught that Russian was the key to a cosmopolitan humanity, to fulfilling culture, sophistication, personal success, and power. They had been told Romanian was a foreign language they could not understand spoken by a culture that was inherently fascist. Little wonder they were confused.

At first I was puzzled by the penchant of Romanian-language publications in Moldova to print interviews with visiting personalities from Romania that invariably began with an exchange that went as follows.

"When you visit Moldova, can you understand what people say to you?"

"Yes, of course, I understand everything. We speak the same language."

This observation, self-evident to any foreigner who had worked his way through a Romanian grammar book and practised with a few language cassettes, was revolutionary in the climate of post-Soviet Moldova. When, gasping for a word, I seized a book with the title *Romanian-English Dictionary* printed on the cover, Andrei's mother dealt me a dismissive wave. I wouldn't find Moldovan words there! But I did. When the procedure worked the next time, and the next, Dora's heavy face settled into a perplexed expression. The year before she had gone to visit a friend who had moved to Romania, and had made herself understood without effort. But she still couldn't bring herself to acknowledge that the language she spoke was Romanian. She was forty-one years old, and such a recognition would overturn the foundations of her life, her intimate, if troubled, sense of herself as a Moldovan.

The section of the Buiucani district where Andrei's family lived occupied the crown of a hill on the outskirts of Chişinău. The city's last row of high-rise blocks lay less than ten minutes' walk away; beyond stretched fields of sunflowers and corn. In the opposite direction, looking back over the centre, hills studded with apartment blocks and softened by the cushions of massed treetops, punctured by the occasional glimmering oval of a small lake, tumbled away toward the lower, flatter downtown portion of Ştefan Cel Mare Boulevard. From my family's apartment I could stare out at the lined-up dominoes of identical high-rise blocks. The development contained between twenty and thirty such buildings, nearly all of them nine stories high. Files of buildings met at right angles, dividing the spaces between them into common areas containing dusty playgrounds, concrete walkways, half-buried tractor tires, stray benches arrayed beneath scarce trees, rudimentary swing sets, and a parking lot. Around the fringes of some of the common areas, and out on the street in front of the development, kiosks that stayed open late sold booze to armies of nocturnal drinkers.

Each building contained apartments of different sizes. Lower-middle-class people lived in two-room apartments, middle-class people in three-room apartments, and wealthy people in four-room apartments. (This calculation omitted kitchens, which were usually tiny.) Andrei's parents, the Lencuţas, were middle-class. Senya Lencuţa was a lawyer, and Dora had worked at shop counters. As I entered their apartment, there were three doors on the right and one, at the back of the flat, on the left. The first door on the right opened onto the living room, the second onto the narrow slot of the kitchen, and the third onto a small TV room, which at night became Andrei's bedroom. The door on the left led into the master bedroom, which was roughly the same size as the modest living room. Andrei shared this apartment with his parents and his blond nine-year-old brother, Sergiu, known as Serge. Four people in three rooms was a luxurious allotment of space by Moldovan standards; the Lencuţas had decided they had plenty of extra room to take in an English teacher.

I was going to be sleeping in the living room. Long couches, meeting in an L, lined two walls of the room. The wall opposite the larger couch was blocked from sight by a huge wall unit concealing a multitude of shelves and cupboards behind glossy imitation-wood doors. The wall opposite the smaller couch was a French window leading to a tin-roofed balcony with a sweeping seventh-floor view of rows of high rises hinged at right angles, dusty yard space and, discernible in the gaps between the buildings, the blurred green horizons of faraway hills. The living room was dominated by a very large black television sitting asquat a high table in front of the French window at an angle making the screen watchable from both couches. The larger couch, its cushions and armrests a startling purple velvet, unfolded into the bed where I was to sleep. Searching for a space where I could keep my clothes and books, Dora flipped up a section of the couch hooding a small compartment. Her shoulders stiffened against the fabric of her voluminous blue-patterned summer dress. It was obvious the space, filled with immaculately folded sheets, wasn't big enough for my belongings. But what had brought her up short, lying on top of the sheets, was a framed colour photograph.

The photograph showed three smiling, close-set faces—woman, man, child. The fierce, low-browed man was Andrei. Then I realized it couldn't be Andrei because the black-haired, pugnacious child was patently a near-infant Andrei. The woman was lean, angular, Slavic-looking, her blond hair thick; only the curl of her smile allowed me to grasp that this was how Dora had looked at twenty-five. The man, bearing such an eerie resemblance to Andrei, could only be...

Dora and Andrei stood in hunched silence. Andrei, staring straight down at the oversize curlicues of the pattern in the carpet, seemed distraught. Dora met my eyes with an ashamed expression. "Domnul Steve," she said, "I had another family before this family. But there were problems in this family. Later I married Senya, who is a good papi... Andrei's little brother has a different father from Andrei."

Dora looked mortified. Andrei's robust body had deflated, his shoulders sagging.

"I understand," I said. "For us this is normal. My brother and I have different mothers."

"It happens in your countries, as well?" Dora asked. "I thought you didn't have these problems."

"It happens everywhere. Some marriages don't work."

The atmosphere was transformed. Dora smiled and cleared two shelves in the wall unit for me with exuberant sweeps of her arms. I unpacked my clothes and books, while Andrei watched to see what treasures I would disgorge. Dora picked out those of my shirts appropriate for teaching and took them away to wash and iron. Later that summer Dora made guarded allusions to her first husband's heavy drinking and "bad behaviour," which I took to mean either infidelity or domestic violence. The family dynamics helped explain Andrei's attachment to Russian culture. Dora had been born into a large Romanian-speaking family in Călăraşi, a town about halfway between Chişinău and the Romanian border whose inhabitants had a reputation for toughness and obstinacy. She had moved to Chişinău as a young woman after completing high school. In Chişinău Dora had met and married Andrei's father, a Ukrainian named Kaminskiy. During Andrei's infancy, the family lived in Ukraine. After her divorce, Dora moved back to Moldova with her son. I couldn't help but see Andrei's cultivation of Slavic values, his worshipful allegiance to Soviet institutions, as his ways of conserving his link with his vanished father.

I met Andrei's stepfather that evening. Simion Lencuţa, who shortened his name to the Russian diminutive Senya, strutted in the door in a pale blue short-sleeved shirt, carrying a black leather purse in his hand. Senya was nearly a dwarf. Less than a metre and a half tall, he barely reached to his wife's armpits. The hard, beetle-shell curve of his belly, starting nearly at his throat, had sucked the vitality out of the rest of his body. His arms, though not misshapen, looked feeble; his legs appeared as brittle as fossils. He was fifty-four years old, his lightly greying hair was parted on one side like that of a politician, and his features were handsome and regular. Dora suggested that he sit down and chat with me. He asked me my age. I told him

I was thirty-four. "In Moldova," he said, "a man your age would look older."

My age had taken the family by surprise: they had been expecting a student. I explained I had recently returned to being a student after having worked for a number of years. "Sometimes in our society it's necessary for adults to get new qualifications," I said. "Anyway, we all get old."

"*Da.*" Senya echoed my words: "*Toți îmbătrinesc.*" His ironic smile barely nudged a face that had dulled and stiffened. Life had not been easy for Senya. He had been born the youngest of five children in a small town near Bălți, Moldova's second-largest city, in the north of the country. His mother had died when he was an infant, in 1942 or 1943, a casualty of World War II. Senya had grown up deformed. In the sweltering Moldovan summer, where nearly all men went shirtless at home, Senya was never dressed in less than a T-shirt, not even when toiling over the stove in the tiny, steaming kitchen. He was an excellent cook. I asked him about this one day and he replied that he had cooked for himself from childhood until his mid-forties when he married Dora. Senya was a sly, intelligent, surprisingly assertive man who suffered from bouts of peevish ill temper; in despair he could become melodramatic. As a lawyer, he earned a good salary: one hundred and thirty lei a month. (At this time there were four Moldovan lei to the U.S. dollar.) His work as a public defender frustrated and embittered him, forcing him to spend his days in the company of muggers, prostitutes, and recidivist drunks. Gratingly articulate and fascinated by politics, Senya might have parlayed his legal training into more active political involvement had he been of ordinary stature. He read Romanian fluently and seemed to be equally at home in the Latin and Cyrillic alphabets. I was not what he had expected when he agreed to take an English teacher into his home—too old, too knowing, too intrusive in my probing—but like Dora, Andrei, and Serge, he welcomed me with impeccable hospitality. Later, speaking to other English teachers, I realized that the language barrier had caved open a gulf between them and their host families. Communicating mainly through sign language, they had gleaned little of family dynamics, jobs, financial worries, political tensions. I was lucky. Conversation hastened familiarity. After a week, I felt as if I were becoming a Moldovan.

Not all aspects of family life made for easy adaptation. I had less space and privacy than I was used to. In fact, the Lencuţa family had little conception of personal privacy in the sense that middle-class Westerners understood the term. Their confined living quarters didn't permit such caprices. Andrei's bedroom was also the lounge and sewing room. On a couple of afternoons I saw Dora and her friends go into the room to chat and sew, apparently oblivious to the fact that Andrei, having worked overnight on some passing odd job, lay asleep and undressed on his unfolded sofa bed. Likewise, at five-thirty or six in the morning, I would be awoken by members of the family, in varying states of near-nakedness, trailing nonchalantly into the living room to retrieve some item of clothing from the wall unit.

The apartment's interior doors were fitted with full-length panels of translucent glass embossed with light, leaf-patterned whorls. A single lamp turned on anywhere in the apartment infiltrated all rooms; someone standing in front of your door could see your every movement. The first morning that I rolled out of bed to dress only to realize Dora and Serge were standing in the hall before my door, I hesitated. I soon learned to ignore such presences: unflustered themselves by the notion of dressing in front of others, the Lencuţas would not have understood my reserve.

This casualness, though, was emphatically limited to a well-defined family sphere. Moldova was conspicuously innocent of such Western decadences as nude sunbathing, *Penthouse*-style magazines, or porno-graphic—or even mildly sexy—films. In questions of sexual morality, Chişinău was the most puritanical city I had visited. Andrei, at twenty, was forbidden to invite individual female friends into the apartment even when his parents were present.

Exhausted by my trip, I slept heavily my first nights in Chişinău, waking late to a busy apartment. At five-thirty in the morning, no matter how scrupulously I had closed the balcony door, the mosquitoes massing outside would buzz into the room, deviously picking out the most painful and persistently itchy places to bite: elbows, knuckles, shins. Slapping and scratching, I would finally doze off again. One of the first words I added to my rapidly growing Romanian vocabulary was *ţânţar*. The dictionary translation was *gnat*, but no gnats ever bit like the early-morning mosquitoes of Chişinău. Another English teacher, who was sleeping on her family's enclosed balcony, later developed such a severe reaction to her *ţânţar* bites that she had to be treated with what we called "the dreaded green stuff"—a verdantly luminous, almost indelible disinfectant in which all cuts were promptly lathered. The shamrock blotches lingered on children's arms and legs—as on my colleague's limbs—for weeks after other evidence of cuts, scratches, or bites had disappeared.

I began to feel trapped. The taxi ride from the train station had tantalized me with glimpses of a glittering southern city. It was days before I was permitted another visit to the centre; I had to wait nearly a week until I had the opportunity to explore on my own. I felt isolated and restless. For the first few days Dora and Senya refused to let me leave the apartment unescorted. Chişinău, they maintained, was a big city (the population was about seven hundred thousand)— too big for foreigners to amble about on their own. I replied that I wasn't planning to rove around at night. I simply wanted to see the centre of the city, take the occasional walk around the neighbourhood. They shook their heads. I tried to explain that I was an experienced traveller: I had lived in Bogotá, Colombia; I had explored on my own from Morocco to Rio de Janeiro; I had survived a Shining Path liberated zone in Peru and visited northern Nicaragua during the *contra* war. None of this made any impression on them. I reached for cities nearer at hand. Warsaw, for example. I had walked around Warsaw at night, so why not Chişinău in the daytime? Senya and Dora closed ranks. Warsaw was a much more civilized city. It had never been part of the Soviet Union; people weren't as crooked and desperate as they were in Chişinău.

I lost the argument and remained stuck in the apartment, writing in my journal and studying Romanian grammar. Defying Senya and Dora's interdiction would destroy my relationship with the family. Moldovan family structure was inflexible. If I wished to obtain a margin of freedom, I would have to secure it in the same way Moldovans acquired the rare pockets of pleasure, privilege, or indulgence in their lives: through patience and stealth; by blending collaboration with deception rather than by rebelling.

I could leave the apartment only if Andrei consented to accompany me. Andrei wasn't much given to walks. Employed as a television salesman, he preferred to sit in his room where his wares, encased in cardboard boxes, were piled against the walls. He watched MTV in English from Amsterdam, or Hollywood movies in which the dialogue had been muted and overlaid with a monotone Russian explanation of the characters' words and actions. When the telephone rang, Andrei jumped. *"Dobrý dien,"* he would growl into the receiver, hoping one of the advertisements he placed in commercial papers had yielded a buyer. Most of the phone calls, though, seemed to be from Dora's friends or Senya's clients. On a few occasions I heard Andrei eagerly announcing the television's brand name and—I assumed—its other features in loud Russian, but during my first week in the family, no client came to the door.

The Lencuţas' refusal to allow me to go out stemmed in part from their utilitarian approach to life. Why did I need to go out? Leaving the apartment meant spending money on transportation, being squashed by the sweating crowds in the trolley bus, wrangling with shopkeepers over scarce goods. Never having been able to travel, they couldn't understand the idea of wandering around a city for pleasure. What did I want to *do* downtown? My failure to provide a satisfactory reply to this question provoked confusion and even suspicion.

Perhaps I wished to slip away and do something unspeakable? I finally decided I needed to buy postcards and a map. Andrei stoutly told me that city maps did not exist. Faced with my chafing eagerness to escape, Dora finally ordered Andrei to take me downtown for an hour.

Andrei and I rode the trolley bus down the long slope into the centre, then up the hill along Ştefan Cel Mare Boulevard, past the Parliament, the spaceship-like former Communist Party headquarters, the elegant parks, the Arc de Triomphe, the sturdy shops. The sun was shining and crowds of people filled the streets. Men selling ice cream that gurgled out of silvery metal vats at the press of a button were fending off customers all along the boulevard. I felt exhilarated, but Andrei soon grew irate. What was I looking for? He didn't understand the Romanian word for postcard, offering in response a Russian word I didn't know. "What do you want to do?" he asked as I ambled from shop to shop, fascinated by the long counters, the teams of saleswomen who handed goods to customers for examination, the rattling abacuses on which checkout women calculated change at bewildering speed. Before I could locate a city map or postcards, Andrei put his foot down. "Steve, we have to go home."

We went home. A few days later Dora and Serge accompanied me downtown for the introductory meeting of the teachers, where we were to be briefed on Moldovan culture and given our teaching assignments. Our supervisor, a stern, elderly woman, addressed us in correct, stilted English. "Here in Moldova we are between Europe and Asia. For many years we were trying to build socialism. Now we have stopped building socialism and we do not know what we are trying to build." She went on to warn us against drunkenness and licentiousness. Moldovans were very conservative people; we must respect their morality. Besides, Chişinău was a dangerous city: if you walked around drunk, you could get beaten up and robbed. She verified our credentials; having more teaching experience than my colleagues, I was handed the job of teaching secondary school and college teachers of English. My job was very prestigious, the supervisor explained, but also potentially difficult. "You must be very strict with them," she said. "Each one is used to being a little dictator."

Dora and Serge waited for me outside the classroom. "Have you finished, Steve?" Dora asked. "Now we will cross the street and take the trolley bus home."

We had stepped out of the school where the meeting had taken place into a gleaming park. "I would like to take a walk downtown," I said.

The supervisor, walking near us, intervened in Romanian. "Did you understand what Doamna Dora said, Steve? You are going home now."

*"Da, am înţeles."* I had understood but continued to console myself with dreams of how I would range around the city in freedom once I had begun teaching and gained the liberty to spend the day away from Buiucani. At a stroke I had grasped why writers from Prague eastward, whether Slavic, Jewish, Magyar, or Romanian, whether living under Habsburgs, tsars, commissars, or post-Communist successor states, had sustained such a consistently rich vein of fantastic writing. Regardless of ideology, these societies' authoritarian ethics, filtering down into family life, thwarted personal fulfillment at such a basic level that the flight into fantasy became a vital recourse for maintaining mental equilibrium. The more autocratic the oppression, the more extravagant the fantasy required to compensate for it.

This insight dovetailed with a mental technique I had begun to evolve over the past few days to make up for the absence of private space. Once I had folded up my bed in the morning, there was no spot in the apartment defined as mine—no place I could be alone. By my third day with the Lencuţas, I found I could summon up a whirling cordon of privacy within my head, warding off the intrusive voices, movements, and presences of other people by submerging myself in a hoop of inner space whose boundaries I could press outward around me like a magnetic field. When I sat at the living-room table writing in my travel journal, no one else existed. The phenomenon, though essential to my mental and emotional well-being, disconcerted me. I had always paid close attention to the world around me. Growing up on a farm where space abounded, I could hide away when I wished to read or write or brood. Once I returned from hiding, I expected to engage with humanity. The habit of periodically shutting out all others, though in Moldovan society as necessary to any sensitive person as dreams were to sleep, struck me alternately as callous and irresponsible. Scrutinizing passengers on the jammed trolley buses, where sweating bodies squeezed against me from all sides, I thought I saw others switching on their mental cordons as I was learning to activate mine.

Like most fantasies, mine remained unrealized. The beginning of my job failed to release me into freedom. I was teaching at the Technical University in the Botanică district at the opposite end of Chişinău from Buiucani. An early-morning commuter express bus carried me the length of the city. I taught from nine to twelve, then rode a local bus back to Ştefan Cel Mare Boulevard, where I could soak up urban life, shop (I soon found both a city map and post-cards), change money, or idle with other English teachers who spent afternoons sitting on benches behind the statue of Stephen the Great at the entrance to Ştefan Cel Mare Park. Whatever I did, I had to do it quickly because Dora expected me home for lunch. Senya didn't come home for lunch, but Andrei did. At one or one-thirty Andrei, Dora, and I would squeeze around the kitchen table and eat. If I got delayed, Dora would become angry. If the delay were prolonged, she would be furious. One day I returned at five-thirty to be met by Dora stepping into the hall to present me with a plate of food. "Your lunch!" she said. "Steve, *la masa*! To the table!"

I sat and ate. Two hours later I sat again and ate supper. After that I never returned to Buiucani any later than two in the afternoon. Contact with my colleagues dwindled. I was becoming part of a Moldovan family.

# 3

# THE JACKSONS
# ARE COMING!

The Friday evening before my course began Andrei took me for a walk around the development. We crossed the dusty, rectangular lots where daytime social life unfolded. In the dark I could make out concrete walkways, upright tractor tires half buried in the earth, rudimentary swing sets, stray benches and picnic tables, and large iron-tube frames over which women draped rugs in order to beat them clean. Groups of men supplied with vodka from the kiosks around the fringes of the development sat playing cards at the picnic tables listing into the night's deep shadows. Only the solitary parking lot was lighted. Andrei told me the neighbourhood was safe at night for groups or pairs of men, though not for single people; during the day, it was safe for more or less anyone, a fact of which he and his friends were proud.

Andrei asked me about "business." Speaking no English, he would nonetheless spit out this word in a semblance of its English pronunciation, spiking it with trappings of machismo, streetwise knowledge, manly self-possession. Andrei had attended Russian-language schools, graduating from a technical high school with an auto mechanic's diploma. He had worked only briefly in this field (jobs soon dried up) and, for someone twenty years of age, had notched up a bewildering variety of work experience: housepainting, construction work in Moscow, harvest-time labour in Romania, unspecified tasks in Ukraine, dozens of attempts to do "business" in Chişinău and Tiraspol by buying, selling, and transporting different types of merchandise. Business, he was convinced, would be his salvation. "You set up a good business, Steve, and...no more problems!"

He desperately wanted me to confirm that business was the answer, that an answer existed—a solution to the dead end in which he was trapped. The Soviet Union had rewarded acquiescence with total security. Andrei remained convinced that this new social organization, which he understood to be based around business, would provide him with a similar degree of security in much greater opulence, if only he could master the system. The notion that the essence of this new system lay in the withdrawal of security had not penetrated his mind. In this, I suspected, he was far from alone. What would happen when the Andreis of the planet realized that "business" wasn't a more lavish method of organizing society, but an order under whose sway society, in Margaret Thatcher's words, did not exist? My responses, in any event, were too Western for him: "You never have complete security. You always have to change and adapt."

This was unacceptable. "Steve, I've been working on a plan for three years that will make everybody so rich we'll never have to work again. Before you leave Moldova I'll make you a very interesting business proposition!"

He had been alluding to this plan since my arrival, vowing to share the details with me. He could barely contain himself.

As we walked around the development, young men would detach themselves from loitering groups and come over to speak to us. Andrei and I shook hands with each young man in turn. Most of the youths wore the baggy blue track suits with red, white, and green stripes running down the side that were the uniform of the young male in Chişinău. On their feet they wore rubber sandals. Sports shoes, I had learned, were a luxury item and a rarity; my brief sally onto Ştefan Cel Mare Boulevard had alerted me to the intrigued stares aroused by my Reeboks. Once the greetings were complete, Andrei's conversations with the youths would lapse into Russian. After the first of these conversations, Andrei apologized for speaking in a language I didn't understand. *"Ruseşte e mai bine pentru business."*

Andrei and his friends, I was discovering, were not alone in this belief. All over Moldova, Russian seemed to be regarded as "better for business." In less than four years the language had achieved a remarkable metamorphosis. From the bearer of socialist ideology, Russian had transformed itself into the symbol of mass-market modernity, second only to English—a language spoken by virtually no one in Moldova—as the associate of glorious consumerism. The riddle of how to attain the consumerist paradise enjoyed by Westerners and successful members of the Russian Mafia stymied young Moldovans. Andrei's dilemma turned out to be typical, not unique. With the exception of a couple of part-time teachers, I would meet no one in Moldova under the age of thirty-five who could be described as gainfully employed. Like Andrei, most of his contemporaries spent the day marvelling at the riches paraded on MTV, their dreamy boredom punctuated by occasional bouts of buying and selling and carrying goods from one place to another. These sorties propped up personal dignity, but no one got rich on them; the meagre profits realized by, say, buying cheap textiles in Ukraine and selling them at a higher price in Romania were usually sucked away by the cost of train tickets, accommodation, food, and bribes paid to border guards.

Constrained by a fearsome austerity under which jobs and many consumer goods—nearly any merchandise, in fact, other than vodka or bread—had vanished, Andrei nevertheless assigned the blame for the lousy economy to inflation. The subject came up via the back door. I was asking him about language; I had mentioned that his little brother, Serge, attended a Romanian-language school. Andrei scoffed. "Romanian school! That's a thing of the 1990s. It won't last. Steve, you have to understand there used to be a great empire that included Russia, Ukraine, Belarus, and Moldova. But that fell apart and now we all have inflation."

Moldova, in fact, did not suffer from severe inflation: the leu remained rock-steady at four to the U.S. dollar. The country's problem was stagnation, not overstimulation; economic activity had ground to a standstill. Andrei's adoption of careering Russian and Ukrainian inflation as his own had been absorbed from Russian television. His colonization was so deep he couldn't see the reality around him. Andrei's bamboozlement reminded me of Canadians sedated by U.S. television who slapped U.S. names onto Canadian institutions. Not wanting to challenge him too overtly, I murmured, "Is inflation a very big problem in Moldova?"

"Not with a good *business!*" he said, again driving the English word through his Romanian sentence. "Steve, I'm going to tell you my plan. Listen carefully. I've spent three years working on this idea."

We had emerged onto a patch of sunken concrete; the high rises around us stood on bald, pitted hillocks. Andrei was walking in a posture of hunched determination, emphasizing the shortness and heaviness of his body. He peered forward from beneath his profuse black brows, concentrating with rapt attention on the future he hoped to summon from the shadows.

Speaking very quickly, Andrei said, "There is a fight in a family. A horrible fight. We show this onstage. Then the damage is healed. And the Jackson family comes and makes it better by giving a huge concert. I mean, a concert here in Chişinău by the whole Jackson family—Michael, Jermaine…"

"But, Andrei—"

"No, Steve, I've spent three years working on this idea. I know people in the music business. I know there's a market for this. That's why I was happy when Papi said we were getting an English teacher to stay with us. You can use your English to talk to the Jacksons and get them to come."

"I can't talk to the Jacksons just because I speak English. It's like me asking you to use your Russian to talk to Boris Yeltsin."

"You can do it, Steve! I'll cut you in and you'll be rich. You'll never have to work again. Just think—Michael Jackson will come to Chişinău with his whole family!"

I realized that, on top of everything else, his wholesome vision of the Jacksons was sadly dated. "Andrei, Michael Jackson has had a lot of problems recently. Health problems…" I tried to think of a way of mentioning the allegations that Jackson had molested adolescent boys. But in Chişinău this remained the scandal that dared not speak its name. I finally said, "His reputation is not good now."

"I don't care about that, Steve. I just want the Jacksons to come to Chişinău. The whole family…"

"I can't help you do that, Andrei."

My relationship with Andrei never fully recovered from this disappointment. We were back on good terms in a few days, but from that evening onward his exuberance alternated with a tone of corrosive bitterness. I had failed him. I wondered about the psychological implications of his fantasy, which struck me as embarrassingly transparent. The family quarrel that was to open the spectacle seemed to represent both his parents' divorce and the splintering of the Soviet Union— the two events had grown nearly synonymous for Andrei—while the advent of the Jacksons, who were both a mass-media chimera and, crucially, a family, provided reassurance that the new globalized order would act to restore life to its former stability. The family unity—of the Soviet Union and of Andrei's Romanian mother and Ukrainian father within that confederation—would be anointed by the blessing of an MTV deity. Again the message that global mass culture brought the dissolution of fixed values and identities had failed to get through. Andrei was trying to go back to the future where the endurance of the Soviet family unit would be consecrated in the glare of halogen lamps, the puff of smoke bombs, and the whine of synthesizers. His need and desperation were tragic, but I didn't think it was fair to allow his illusions to persist.

We returned to the apartment in forbidding silence. Andrei went out to drink with friends at a picnic table in the dark. The next evening he disappeared as soon as supper ended. On the weekend before my course began he made himself scarce, effectively marooning me in the apartment. I had failed to live up to the image of a Westerner as he had been taught to regard the species by MTV. Not only was I incapable of communicating with the Jacksons, but my knowledge of the dollar prices of different models of cars, different brands of televisions and VCRs and Walkmans, was pathetically deficient. Andrei and his friends revelled in discussions of the finer points of such gadgets. Although none of them owned Walkmans or VCRs (they all had televisions), they had memorized the differences between different makes and models. I had been expected to supply crucial dollar figures to amplify their discussions. But I proved hopeless at telling them how much each model of each gadget would cost in England/America, which was all one place—the land where MTV happened.

As a Westerner, I was an unnerving disenchantment.

Dora and Senya saved me from being stuck in the apartment all weekend by inviting me for a walk. They attributed Andrei's disappointment with me to the difference in our ages. As we crossed the corner of the development leading toward open fields of corn and sunflowers, Dora and Senya took pains to treat me as an equal. Senya, with old-fashioned courtesy, addressed me as "Domnul Steve"—"Mr. Steve." They spoke to me slowly and corrected the mistakes in my Romanian, apparently proud to be teaching me their language. As we walked, I realized the development was far larger than I had imagined; it contained two schools, a hotel, a post office, a restaurant and bar, and numerous sports facilities, though very little grocery shopping. That morning I had noticed that most of the newspapers sold by the kiosks along the edge of the road where people from the development caught their buses downtown to work were printed in the Cyrillic alphabet. I had bought a Latin-alphabet paper called *Europa*. On opening it up I discovered to my dismay that though the front page was in Latin letters, most of the articles inside, though written in the Romanian language, were printed in the Cyrillic alphabet. The linguistic situation grew more and more confusing. "Do most people here speak Romanian…Moldovan?" I asked Senya.

"Most people speak Moldovan and Russian. Moldovans speak Russian, but Russians don't speak Moldovan. But I don't want to push the Russians living here out of Moldova. Many of them are old and sick. They were given apartments here in the south because they were wounded in the war in Afghanistan, or they came here to retire. The real swine are the Germans. *Deutschenschwein!*"

His digression took me by surprise; he was shaking with rage. For an instant I thought the story of what had happened to his family during World War II was about to tumble out. But Dora laid her hand on his shoulder. She pointed to a large, flat-roofed, single-story building. "That's Serge's school, the Romanian gymnasium. Andrei went to the Russian school. He's a little Russian. For him everything is in Russian and Ukrainian. He hardly uses Moldovan." Dora presented their decision to send Serge to Romanian school as a considered response to this outcome.

The next day, when my supervisor phoned to give directions to the Technical University where I would teach, Andrei asked her to switch into Russian. Having written down the directions in Russian, he proved nearly incapable of translating them into Romanian. He had to ask Senya the words for *avenue, architecture building*, and *engineering building*. His transcription into the Latin alphabet mixed up *b*'s and *d*'s. Serge would never make these mistakes; Romanian history and literature would be his heritage.

On the way back to the apartment Senya and Dora asked me about my rent in Montreal. They told me an apartment such as theirs cost US$2,000 to buy. Dora pointed out a white apartment block from which the paint wasn't peeling. I noticed large enclosed balconies that projected outward rather than being recessed into the building, as was common in Central and Eastern Europe. The lower levels of the building were overgrown with thick creepers. "Three bedrooms, a living room, *and* a kitchen," Dora said. "Those apartments cost $13,000." A friend of Dora's who had moved across the border to Romania, having decided that life was better there, was trying without success to unload one of these expensive apartments. Not many Moldovans had $13,000 to spend on real estate. "It would be very easy for you to buy an apartment here, Steve," Dora said. "You could save money in your country, buy a couple of apartments in Chişinău, rent one out, then live very easily here as an English teacher."

"That's true," I said. In strictly financial terms she was correct, though I suspected that Soviet laws banning foreigners from owning property were still on the books. Had Dora offered me the solution to my eternal dilemma of financing my need to write? I struggled to convey to her that what I would miss living in Moldova would be contact with my own culture, with my language, with Canadian political and literary debates. My explanations confused Dora and Senya. The pulverization of their culture had diminished the value they placed on the notion of belonging. As accustomed to trading in identities as they were to bartering old trolley-bus tickets, they couldn't imagine how anyone could miss his homeland when an easier life beckoned elsewhere.

# 4

# LITTLE DICTATORS

Botanică, near the highway leading to the airport, was a spaciously conceived district of tall 1960s towers bounded by broad avenues and buffers of greenery. The layout diverged sufficiently from the gridlike East Bloc norm that at a distance certain vistas could have been mistaken for the high-rise-studded outskirts of a Canadian city. The home of professionals and middle-level bureaucrats, the neighbourhood had been popular among the Jewish community until the Jews began to leave Moldova in the early 1990s. As I rode in on the bus from the city centre, the high rises lining the multi-lane streets looked impressive. A short walk tempered this vision. Grass sprouted through the cracks in the sidewalk, and most of the shops were as empty as those elsewhere in the city, though a few stores sold luxury goods, such as a rare box of orange juice priced at one-tenth of a teacher's monthly salary. The campus of the Technical University was pocked with the pits of unfinished construction work.

The little dictators were all women. Men refused to teach in Moldova because the salary was too low: eighty lei a month. (Due to the country's near-bankruptcy, teachers hadn't been paid for the past four months.) The English spoken by my students, most of whom were between twenty-five and forty-five years old, was highly proficient. They taught the language at well-regarded specialist institutions and good Russian-language high schools. The younger ones were all teaching part-time. They seemed to be roughly equally divided between native speakers of Russian and Romanian—the group's composition fluctuated over the summer—though none of them taught at Romanian-language schools. A policy persisting from Soviet days, when official doctrine had decreed that the "structures of the Moldovan brain" made Romanian speakers poorly equipped to learn English, determined that English was taught primarily in Russian-language schools. Students at Romanian-language schools studied French. These policies were starting to change, but in many schools the Soviet patterns persisted.

Despite their extensive experience studying and teaching English, none of my students—with the exception of a woman named Nelly, whose late husband had been an important Communist Party official— had ever set foot in an English-speaking country. Before 1991 they had not been allowed to travel; now they could not afford to do so. Until signing up for this course, many of them had never conversed with a native speaker. They had learned their English from the same Soviet textbook, printed in 1950, which they continued to use in their own classes.

Later in the summer I asked to see a copy of this famous book. It was a small, dowdy, durable hardcover volume. I opened it to a comprehension passage and read: "Mary lives in Manchester. She suffers from the cyclical nature of capitalism. Her father is unemployed..." The assessment didn't seem that unrealistic. The book's language, on the other hand, was stiff, outdated, and sometimes wrong. Accustomed to drilling the book's patterns into students' heads, the teachers reacted fiercely and in unison to transgressions. Occasionally my pronunciation of a word—*nephew* was one such catalyst—would provoke a shouted correction from the entire class: *"Nev-view!"* The authoritarian habit turned them all against one another; if one teacher made a mistake, the others would bombard her with corrections. I had to intervene forcefully to establish that in this class I would do the correcting. Once I had asserted *my* dictatorial authority, the tyrannical ladies became eager to learn. They were all painfully aware that the English they spoke was fast becoming outdated, and had to cope with students addicted to MTV who spouted slang expressions gleaned from rock videos. The experience was undermining their authority—the last shred of dignity left to them in a society that couldn't afford to pay their salaries.

Until my arrival the teachers' course had been taught by Theresa, a retired Irish schoolteacher. Each day we would decide, according to the number of students present, whether to split the class or teach together. My first morning I watched Theresa teach for an hour. Her manner combined an antiquated, more-English-than-the-English quality bred, she informed me, at Trinity College, Dublin, with a well-meaning, earth-grandmother warmth. Her grey hair was cut short but floppy; her baggy skirt eeled with bright colours. "Men sweat," she told the students, commenting on the staggering early-morning heat. "Ladies perspire." She went on to describe the ritual of "a boy asking a girl's father for her hand" as though such behaviour had fallen from fashion only last year. Perhaps in Ireland it had.

I wasn't certain that this sort of vocabulary enrichment would enable the teachers to decipher MTV, but there was no gainsaying Theresa's professionalism. Having set out into the world "to make myself stop moping after my husband died," she retained a charming vagueness about where she had ended up. Tiring of the history of how Stalin and Molotov had sliced out the Republic of Moldova from the Romanian region of Moldavia, she had settled on a personal compromise, referring to the country as "Moldava."

When I began to teach, the students let me speak for ten minutes, murmuring avidly among themselves to agree on Russian translations of the new words I was using. Then they interrupted. "Stephen," one of them said, apparently at the others' behest, "we want you to know how happy we are that you are here. You cannot imagine how wonderful it is for us that you have come to work with us."

"We have been waiting for this moment for fifteen years," another woman said. Her neighbours chorused agreement.

"Thank you very much," I said. "I'm very happy to be in Chişinău. I'm looking forward to working with you."

Their gratitude couldn't be stifled. The large, dusty classrooms were sweltering. My short-sleeved white shirt, which Dora had ironed to military crispness, was soon sodden with sweat. (Men sweat, indeed!) The soapy chalk broke in my hand, its dust settling along the inside of my throat. I grew hoarse and dehydrated. During the next few days, I searched in vain for a reliable source of liquid refreshment. Bottled water and clear soft drinks were unknown; repulsive Coca-Cola and Pepsi, like juice, were intermittently available in a few specialty shops at very high prices; only vodka was omnipresent. I could find no relief. My voice rasped, my head throbbed. My students saved me with their astonishingly bountiful generosity. They hadn't been paid in weeks, their husbands were marginally employed, their children clamoured for necessities they couldn't afford, yet every day they brought me a thermos of lemon tea to preserve my voice, bags of fruit to offset my dehydration, and homecooked Moldovan delicacies to nibble during the morning break.

Introducing me on my first morning, the course supervisor had mentioned I spoke Romanian. This scrap of information intrigued the Romanian-speaking teachers. At the end of the first class I was waylaid en route to the bus stop by an assertive teacher named Natasha. In a commanding voice that brooked no dissent, she told me we were going to ride downtown together.

Natasha was the most culturally Romanian of my students. She was a sturdy woman in her early forties. Her long, thick black hair was flecked with grey, and the set of her eyes betrayed a slight Asiatic tilt. Her family came from a village across the river from the ugly industrial city of Galaţi, Romania; had they been living five kilometres farther west, they would have escaped Soviet rule. Five kilometres farther and Natasha wouldn't have been named Natasha. By the time she was born in the early 1950s, assimilation was well under way, and few parents were willing to convert their children into targets of oppression by giving them Romanian names. The combination of Natasha's Slavic first name and Latinate Romanian surname might sound incongruous to an outsider, but in Moldova it was normal. A man I met later in the summer told me that in his village's primary school all the Romanian boys in his year were named Vladic because word had gotten around among local Romanian parents that this was a name looked upon with favour by the Soviet authorities.

Natasha, alone among the five children in her family, had escaped the countryside and gone to university. Only the youngest of my students had grown up in Chişinău: among those over thirty, the Romanian speakers had come from the countryside and the Russian speakers had come from elsewhere in the former Soviet Union. (Nelly, unusually, had grown up in Tiraspol.) The pattern rehearsed the history of the deportation of the Romanian middle class and its replacement with a middle class drawn from the Slavic heartland. As we loitered in the dusty, shaded patches where trees grew in gaps in the sidewalk paving, waiting for the arrival of a bus offering enough free space for us to squeeze onboard, Natasha said, "That's one of our biggest problems. We have no leadership. All our potential leaders died in Siberia and their children grew up as Russian-speaking Siberians."

"Did you learn Russian in your village?"

"I learned Russian when I was twelve." Learning Russian had been a crucial stage, the essential qualification for attending university and entering the urban world. Without fluent Russian she would have remained a peasant, condemned to back-breaking labour in a remote village. "It was very difficult for me to learn a Slavic language. I had to work very, very hard. But this has made my life more interesting. I've been able to read the literature. The Russians have the greatest literature in the world. You'll never know what you're missing unless you learn this language…"

Once we had clambered up the steps of a low-slung, fume-spewing bus, shouldering a niche for ourselves out of the cushion of sweating bodies, Natasha's mood darkened. Her full-volume bitterness unnerved me. Could we safely assume no one on the bus understood English?

"I have Russian friends here. Very nice Russians, but if you tell them about the Romanian language, about Romanian literature, they don't want to hear about it. They don't want to admit that you speak this language and they will never learn the language themselves. How can people be like that? How can you go to live somewhere and not learn the language? They say Romanian is an irrelevant language. Well, my parents went to live in the south, among the Gagauz people, and they learned to communicate in Gagauz. Gagauz is a very small language, maybe two hundred thousand people speak this language, but if you go to live with those people, you should learn their language!"

The blast of English staked bodies rigid, raised resentful stares. The theme trembling behind Natasha's last statement was the political tension surrounding the upcoming revision of Moldova's language law. This was an explosive issue, and I was relieved when Natasha waited until we had gotten off the bus on a busy side street near Ştefan Cel Mare Boulevard before bringing it up.

In 1989, as the Moldavian Soviet Socialist Republic began to assert its autonomy within the Soviet Union, a tumultuous public debate ushered in new language laws. Russian ceased to be the province's official language. While retaining the Soviet-era term *Moldovan*, the new laws included a recognition that Moldovan and Romanian were the same language. In essence, the laws enshrined Romanian as Moldova's official language. The country's clocks were set to Bucharest time; the phantom of reunification flickered for a few weeks until *realpolitik* crushed it. Having engineered the overthrow of Nicolae Ceauşescu and manoeuvred Ion Iliescu, his old crony from Moscow State University student politics in 1950 and 1951, into the presidency of Romania, Soviet leader Mikhail Gorbachev leaned on the Romanian president not to push the reunification issue. A few months later Gorbachev was gone, Moldova's post-independence momentum had been lost, and the old hierarchies and old faces had settled down to the business of ruling the country in the old ways under different banners.

The most revolutionary thread of the new language law lay in the stipulation that by 1994 all civil servants must demonstrate working proficiency in Romanian. This was a direct assault on the Russian administrators imported since the 1940s: most of the civil service was Russian, and there were few Russians who could be described as demonstrating a working proficiency in Romanian. At the time of my arrival in Chişinău the language-law deadline was ticking down to its final days. In the aftermath of the civil war in the summer of 1992, when General Lebed had shown his zeal for putting the former Soviet Fourteenth Army at the service of Slavic nationalism, a mass dismissal of the civil service was out of the question. Merely broaching the idea would bring Lebed's tanks charging down Ştefan Cel Mare Boulevard. Even the old politician's trick of extending the deadline would be viewed as an act of aggression by the Russian civil servants and their supporters in Tiraspol and Moscow. Elections held in the wake of Lebed's punishing assault had granted control of the Parliament to parties hostile to reunification. The new chairman of the Parliament, Petru Lucinschi, was an ethnic Romanian who had risen to staggering heights in the Soviet Communist Party, serving as Kremlin chief of ideology as late as 1991. (Lucinschi conducted his Soviet political career under the name Piotr Kirilovich Luchinskiy.) Lucinschi had introduced a new language law, withdrawing Romanian as Moldova's official language; the infinitely adaptable Snegur complied. The country's new official language was going to be...Moldovan. The new language law, however, made no reference to Moldovan being the same as, or even related to, Romanian.

The signal to the Russian population was clear: the status quo ante had come back; the Stalinist position that the people of the republic spoke a backward dialect and couldn't understand Romanian would once more become official policy. Links with Moscow were "natural" again; fledgling trade and cultural ties with Romania were to be allowed to wither. Most Romanian speakers, living in villages in the countryside, displayed a fatalistic acceptance of the reversion to Soviet policy; they had never expected anything to change. Urban Romanian speakers, such as Natasha, were furious.

"This new government is moving everything back to how it was before. On September 1 the official language of the country will no longer be Romanian but Moldovan. This is so stupid. *It's the same language!* Do they really think they can make us forget what we speak? And they're bringing in a new subject in the schools: Moldovan history. The history of Moldova without Moldavia? What will they teach them? When everything changed, the Russians here were afraid, but now they're holding their heads up again."

She told me a story about picking up her daughter at kindergarten in 1986 or 1987 when the environment had become sufficiently liberal that she could safely speak Romanian among friends on the street. Natasha had asked her daughter, in Romanian, to pick up her coat and come home. The teacher had jumped, screaming at her in front of a class of children that as a Soviet citizen she must at all times speak to her daughter in Russian! Natasha had replied that she understood that children spoke Russian in school, but that the language spoken at home was a family matter.

"I don't want things to go back to being like that, Stephen," she said. "Everything has gotten worse in the past few years. We don't know where we're going or what we want. Our politicians just live a very nice lifestyle and don't do anything for the country. Everything gets worse, but I *don't* want things to go back to how they were before. This is better. I can talk to you, for example."

The next day Theresa and I divided the class. Neither of us

noticed until it was too late that all the Romanian speakers had remained with me, prompting the Russian speakers to depart en masse with Theresa. The following day, determined to thwart this pattern, Theresa and I exchanged classes. I was teaching the Russian ladies, defining in sequence a long list of political terms. When we reached the word *nationalist*, Nelly, brought up on the banks of the Dniester River and proud to have lived sixty years in Moldova without having absorbed a word of "Moldovan," spoke without raising her hand. "This is a very ugly philosophy. Three or four years ago there were many nationalists, many intolerant people, in Moldova, but now things are much better."

The other Russian teachers nodded. Encouraged, Nelly said, "Stephen, I think you must learn Russian while you are in Moldova. If you come here, you must learn our language."

"I'm having enough trouble with Romanian," I said. "If I go to Moscow, I'll learn Russian."

I moved on to the next topic in the book. I didn't want to linger on this subject, because my own reactions to life in Chişinău were disturbing me. I found myself hating Russian, tensing up at each glimpse of the Cyrillic alphabet. (In the capital street signs were either bilingual or in Romanian only; elsewhere in the country no money had been found to remove or supplement the old Russian signs.) My customary spongelike absorption of new sounds and words had dried into a rasping hide. My love of Leo Tolstoy, Ivan Turgenev, and other Russian writers became irrelevant. For the first time in my life I was resisting the opportunity to learn words in a new language. By the end of the summer, my Russian vocabulary remained limited to five or six words. The oppressive weight exerted by Russian in Moldova had built up a hard, glowering resistance in me. Nelly's suggestion that I take up Russian made me aware of my new chauvinism. But who could remain impartial and openhearted in such a polarized environment? Could anyone participate in Moldovan society without taking sides?

After class I walked down the street with Theresa, who was staying in the Botanică district. I mentioned Nelly's definition of nationalism. "I was glad Natasha wasn't there."

"You realize that Natasha's husband had to flee the country for a few months?" Theresa said. "He's a sociologist. He writes about Moldava. About what the Russians have done here." She sighed. "I worry about Natasha's outspokenness. I suggested to her that perhaps this was a time to keep her head down and say nothing. Times will change again." Another pause. "She's been questioning me about you. She can't work out why someone as educated as you is teaching English."

I laughed. "When I think of all the well-educated people I know who have ended up teaching English as a second language!"

But Theresa was serious. "You don't fit the model. And your speaking Romanian confuses them, especially when you say you haven't been to Romania. Natasha's husband would like to meet you, but Natasha wants to be sure which side you're on before she introduces you. She talks about you like something out of *The Spy Who Came in from the Cold*. It's clear some of the others think the same. I thought I'd better let you know."

"Thank you," I said. The whisper of intrigue amused me. I didn't take it very seriously, though I did worry about the ongoing battle of ideologies in my classroom. I finally accepted there was nothing I could do. It was foolish to imagine I could end the squabbling of my little dictators as long as other, more corpulent but equally intransigent dictators ran the country beyond the classroom walls.

# 5

# TOWN, COUNTRYSIDE, AND CAVERNS

Theresa and I were riding a city bus toward the outskirts of Chişinău. Our supervisor had arranged for a group of us to visit the village of Cricova, famous as the centre of Moldova's wine industry. We were to rendezvous at the city circus grounds, where the bus into the countryside departed. As our municipal bus meandered through an increasingly sparse urban fringe, we began to worry that we had missed our stop. I turned to the young couple gripping the railing behind us. "Excuse me," I said in Romanian, "we're looking for the Circus stop. Is it close?"

The young man replied with a burst of Russian. His partner prodded him. *"Moldavski,"* she said.

"Yes," I said. "I'm sorry. I don't know Russian."

*"I don't know Russian."* He mimicked my words with a sneer and turned his back on me.

"That wasn't very successful," I commented to Theresa.

"Maybe we could ask someone else," she said.

Hearing us speak English, the young man turned around, his expression transformed. "You go...end... Circus end," he said in English.

"Thank you very much," I said. The young man beamed. Theresa and I stayed on until the final stop, next to a silvery globelike structure. Our supervisor and a couple of other teachers were waiting for us there. We caught a crowded, coughing bus that hacked its way out of the city into a wide-open landscape where vines clung in trained tiers to the dipping and jutting lines of the prairie. Standing in the bus, we found ourselves surrounded by brawny men whose massive hands were callused beyond any possibility of tactile sensation. The men yelled at each other in Romanian. Twenty minutes out of Chişinău the Russian invasion dissolved and we were back in a Romanian province. The Russian and Ukrainian twenty-seven percent of the population, having supplanted the native urban middle class, had reshaped Chişinău into a distant outpost of the Soviet Union. But the Slavs hadn't penetrated the countryside. Collectivization or no, an antique rural Romania continued to cover most of the national territory.

I noticed the big bruiser next to me eyeing my pretty colleague, Helen, her thick brown hair twisted up in a bun, her attractively tanned shoulders crossed by the straps of her black tank top. A little tipsy, the man tried to strike up a conversation with her. Helen gave him a blank look. I explained that she didn't speak Romanian. The man glanced at me. In a confessional surge he said, "I only speak Romanian."

I was startled. He had referred to the language as *româneşte*. Where an educated, culturally aware urban Romanian speaker such as Senya continued to describe himself as speaking *moldoveanu*, this peasant suffered from no such doubts. He emphasized the point. "Only Romanian! I don't know English. I don't know Russian."

"*Da,*" I said to indicate I had understood. "*Şi eu nu ştiu ruseşte.* I don't know Russian, either."

"*Bravo!*" he said, subjecting my hand to a crushing clasp. At the next stop he got off and headed across the fields.

From disdain to congratulations: not knowing Russian provoked dramatically different reactions in the city and the countryside.

At first sight the village of Cricova didn't look large enough to sustain the wine industry whose products I'd seen stocking shelves as far away as England. Spread over a long, tilted plane of prairie, the village's clusters of pink stucco houses had small, tilled yards enclosed by chest-high walls and front gates padlocked against intruders. The peasants working their private lots in somnambulistic languor were protected by vicious-sounding dogs that lunged against the garden gates as we passed. In spite of the pulverizing sunlight the mud streets felt spongy beneath our shoes. We gasped in relief as we entered the shade of a large, warehouselike building. A guard unchained a service elevator and ushered us inside. We travelled down into the earth. When the doors opened, we held back, startled by the damp cold. The secret of Cricova's significance was that the underground complex was larger than the village on the surface. Above, an early twentieth-century Romanian peasant community; below, a science-fiction netherworld. Passages with tiled walls joined other passages at right angles. Some of these passages were wider than any highway in the country. Many were air-conditioned to a cool moisture that bred an eerie perpetual mist. Huge orange transport trucks would whoosh phantasmagorically out of the mist-glimmered semidarkness, turn a corner, and roar away down another broad passage.

Our tour followed the preparation of Moldovan champagne from grape to bottle. We visited dingy, frigid vaults where kegs were stowed for aging and a brightly lighted assembly-line room where bored bottling workers clowned around to attract our attention. We tramped along endless passages and stepped out of the way of trucks. Our guide told us that Moldova produced the world's only red champagne—drunk, she insisted, by the queen of England. At each stage of the tour we were offered generous samples to taste. I joined in the sampling, though more sparingly than some of my colleagues, who after a couple of hours were barely able to grip their complimentary bottles of Moldovan red wine.

At the end of the tour we were dispatched staggering into the heat at a back service entrance. We found ourselves in a sandy cove in the midst of a pitted landscape less than a kilometre from the centre of the village. A couple in a pickup truck stopped and offered to ferry us back to Cricova. "You've learned our language!" the driver said when I thanked him. "The Russians have been here for fifty years and they still haven't learned our language!"

Returning to the Lencuţas' apartment at six-thirty that evening, I offered my complimentary bottle of wine to Dora. She sat with a circle of women friends, watching a Mexican soap opera dubbed into Russian. Senya, hearing me come in, emerged from the bedroom. "That's Moldova's red gold," he said, spotting the bottle. "The only hard currency this country earns comes from Cricova."

I toured the room, pouring small glasses of wine for Dora's friends, then for Dora, then for Senya. Watching them drink, I felt enclosed in an enduring community. Dora and Senya normally escaped the apartment's evening heat by going to sit *pe scaun* ("on the bench") beneath the sparse L of scrawny trees sketched on the dusty ground dividing their building from the next row of high rises. After visiting Cricova, I came to see the communal life streaming around the wooden benches as a truncated remnant of the wholeness of Romanian village life. Most afternoons Dora and her friends sat out on the benches awaiting the relief of a puff of breeze, caring for and beating one another's children as the tots raced between the frames of swing sets long ago plundered of their swings. Teams of perpetually unemployed young men paced in their track suits, frowning as they discussed doomed "business." As the uniform for young men was track suits and rubber sandals, that for little boys was cutoff shorts and nothing else. Running hard all summer, the little boys turned brown, developing muscular but flat chests resembling squashed, moulded breastplates. The girls, rarely playing outdoors without close maternal supervision, were thin and paler. Girls in Buiucani remained asexually gaunt until they married, at which point their jutting hips and meagre chests decanted voluminous rolls of flesh; at twenty-one they became matrons, as massive as Dora and her friends. As I toured the living room, pouring a second round of Cricova wine, I thought that one of the ways in which I had been luckiest in Moldova was in having been allowed to share this village-like life.

# 6

# DIVIDE AND CONQUER

The afternoon I returned from my first day of teaching Dora offered me a lunch of *greshka*, a heavy, grainy meal enjoyed, she claimed, by Russian soldiers. Exhausted from reining in the little dictators, I collapsed on the living-room couch to digest this coarse, leaden sustenance. I woke three hours later to waning evening heat when Andrei burst into the room to demand that I give him English lessons. English, he had realized, would endow him with an inestimable advantage. English was even better for business than Russian!

I should have grasped that Andrei wouldn't conceive such a plan on his own. An hour later Dora introduced me to Valentina, "a very close acquaintance of ours." Valentina was a dark woman in her early forties, taller than Dora but nearly as stout. The two women sat on one couch and I sat on the other. Valentina, Dora said, laying her hand on her friend's sleeve, had a nine-year-old son named Borislav who had studied English for a year at school....

"Yes, of course, I'll teach him English," I said. "But Andrei also wants to learn. I must be able to teach them both at the same time."

Valentina hesitated. After a long pause, she asked, "Does Andrei know the English alphabet?"

"Yes, he does," I said, though I remembered how he had mixed up his *b*'s and *d*'s. "I'm sorry, but I'm already teaching all morning. I'll teach a class here for one hour at four o'clock every day."

Valentina nodded her acceptance. "How will we pay you?"

The question made me uncomfortable. Any sum she could offer would be derisory to me and prohibitively expensive to her. Profiting from my hesitation, Valentina suggested that in exchange for the classes she give me occasional Romanian conversation classes and at least one weekend drive in the country with her family. *"Foarte bine!"* I said in relief.

My days grew more restricted. The exertion I spent on my tempestuous classes with the little dictators, combined with the bludgeoning heat, tumbled me into a drugged afternoon siesta. Even if I travelled straight back to Buiucani after teaching, I arrived only at one o'clock, finished lunch at two, and generally woke up shortly before four, just in time to prepare for my private lesson. I saw less and less of my British colleagues, who spent the afternoons lounging on benches behind the statue of Stephen the Great or sampling the unbelievably cheap beer (fifty-nine bani—less than twenty-five cents—per large glass) in bars on downtown side streets. Buiucani became my home.

Valentina's son, Borislav, turned up immaculately dressed for his first English class. Instead of Andrei, Serge appeared. Borislav and Serge were the same age, but poor Serge had only studied French at school. Borislav, an appealingly quick and lively but irritating little know-it-all, paraded his superiority mercilessly. We studied numbers and colours and basic expressions with the help of a brightly illustrated Russian textbook one of my colleagues had salvaged from a classroom. Halfway through the hour, Andrei rushed into the living room, ostentatiously shook my hand, and apologized for not joining the class. He swarmed around the apartment for the remainder of the hour, loudly bemoaning the demands made on his time by "business." After three-quarters of an hour, seeing the two little boys growing restless, I prepared to release them a few minutes early. Borislav preempted me. Pointing at the clock, he said in Romanian, "We have eleven minutes left!"

Borislav took after his mother. When Valentina arrived at five o'clock, she said, "Good afternoon, Domnul Steve. Did the class achieve its objectives?"

Her question flabbergasted me. "We've started to achieve our objectives."

"And which of the boys did better?"

The two boys stood at her side, gazing up at me. I couldn't crush Serge by confessing the truth. "Both boys spoke English well."

"But Borislav was better?" Valentina cast her son a threatening look. Borislav stared at me with pleading eyes.

"Borislav has received a better preparation," I said. I was beginning to understand why Andrei had backed out of the class. I pitied Serge.

While I had been teaching, Dora and Senya had been working in the kitchen. Dora emerged with food, Senya with champagne. Unusually, we ate in the living room: it was Valentina's birthday. Everyone drank large quantities of champagne until Senya and Valentina began arguing about whether the Germans (her point of view) or the Russians (his) had started World War II.

During the days that followed, I felt as if Valentina had adopted me. Eager to lose weight, she decided we would combine our Romanian conversation practice with badminton. We threaded a circuitous course between the high rises to a series of asphalt sports courts enclosed by a tall wire-mesh fence where teams of boys played soccer at the far end. Sharing rectangles designed for basketball with boys shooting baskets below bare hoops, we swatted and lunged through the long summer dusk. The birdie sailed up against the backdrop of high-rise blocks, where the bronzed evening light turned silver against the cool, peeling whitewash of the stacked balconies.

Valentina told me that only her mother had been a native speaker of "Moldovan"; her Russian father had been posted to Chişinău after World War II. Valentina's entire education, including a university degree in Kiev, had taken place in Russian. She spoke Romanian rapidly and confidently but feared she would never sound like a native speaker—a fact I had detected from her sometimes confusingly Russified vocabulary and her habit of occasionally using indicative verb forms in sentences that required the subjunctive.

Since the onset of "the problems between the Russian language and the Romanian language" (this was the only time I heard her refer to the language as Romanian), she and her husband had wished to build a little house in Ukraine—a country they expected to be more ethnically tolerant in the years to come than Moldova. "We have to think about the future," she said. "Domnul Borya, my husband, is fifty-three."

The house in Ukraine hadn't come to pass. Valentina, an intelligent, highly ambitious woman who had an administrative job in health care, struck me as thwarted, anxious, and very worried about the multiple perils lying in wait for Borislav as he grew up into the instability of shifting borders and changing ethnic allegiances. Uncertain of her own identity, she didn't care what culture Borislav adopted as long as he was prosperous and safe. "He must learn English!" she insisted. "With English he can go anywhere in the world."

She became possessive of me, at times seeming to compete with Dora for my allegiance in the same way she prodded Borislav to compete with Serge in my classes. At the end of each game of badminton Valentina would drape her arms around my shoulders. The gesture made me uneasy, though it didn't feel at all sexual—more like a desperate clinging to a human outpost of security. At other times Valentina would retreat into an impeccable formality. One evening she turned up at the apartment door, her face clenched into a distraught expression. "Domnul Steve, I am here to apologize for Borislav."

"Pardon?"

"Yesterday he came to your class wearing a dirty shirt. He knows better than to show such disrespect. I want you to know that when he came home and I saw what he had done I beat him for it. It won't happen again."

That weekend Valentina invited me—and Serge—to join a family outing to the countryside. Her *moşul* was visiting from Australia. The word *moş* means *grandfather*, but it can be applied to any elderly male relative; this *moş* was some sort of great-uncle to Valentina. As he hadn't spoken Romanian since 1945, Valentina was eager to have an English speaker along. I was puzzled as to why the presence of an English speaker should be of such grave concern when, as Valentina had made clear, the *moş* spoke Russian. I had forgotten that in the countryside the Russian language evaporated.

Valentina and her husband, Borya, picked us up early on Saturday morning in their four-door Lada sedan. Borya was a grizzled, deeply tanned man with a polite, somewhat forbidding manner. His receding grey hair clung to the top of his head in an embossed, close-cropped shield. We drove down the hill out of Chişinău and past the gates of the ramshackle "black market" where Dora sometimes went to hunt for bargains. Beyond the city limits the land fissured into long, gritty, fin-backed spurs strung between the scattered hills uncoiling from the floors of the dells where small lakes lay still, flat, and glimmering in the early light. The highway rode the back of a raised spur past hillsides of concrete houses lacking windows and in some cases roofs. I stared at the houses. Were they abandoned? Perhaps they were terminally unfinished, like some of the high rises in Buiucani, which had stood untouched since the economic crisis had brought public construction to a halt.

I soon had my answer. Borya parked the Lada against the guardrail overlooking a dry cliff perhaps thirty metres in height. He shucked off his shoes and shirt, exposing a tanned torso knotted with muscle, then padded across the blacktop and led the way down the steep, rocky embankment, his bare feet gripping the stones with prehensile dexterity and a disconcerting imperviousness to pain. I walked alongside him, slipping in my hiking boots. Borya pointed out a row of four skeletal two-story constructions of unfinished brown stone standing in the bottom of the arid ravine, five minutes' walk from one of the small lakelets that people in Moldova referred to as *iaz*. (In Bucharest Romanian a lake is a *lac* and *iaz* means *dam*, but Moldovans, who live closer to the natural world, use both words to describe bodies of water, distinguishing between a *lac* and a *iaz* according to criteria that all Moldovans understand but which I never absorbed.) The houses were lined up along a rough track, bulldozed out of a field, that led up the embankment at a perilously steep angle.

"Our *vila*," Borya said. "People who can afford it have started building *vila*s outside Chişinău to have the things you can't have in the city—space, fresh vegetables. Gorbachev made it legal for us to do this in 1986, but people in Moldova have only started building recently. Most of our money and spare time goes into our *vila*. It'll take us years to finish building…. I had hoped to build in Bulgaria. That's a country that will always be stable. But it was just too expensive."

He shrugged as we emerged onto the bulldozed track. Floundering over the track's deep ruts, I understood why Borya pre-ferred to park on the highway. We turned into the *vila*'s yard, choked with tall, dry cornstalks and the inevitable head-high sunflowers. They were cultivating pears and walnuts amid thick weeds. Borya unlocked the front door; the barren, dirt-floored interior was fur-nished only with piled building supplies. A staircase twirled up into the cavernous gap left by a half-finished second floor. We stepped back into the yard. Tearing at the weeds, Borya and Valentina began to collect cucumbers and tomatoes—their contribution to the meal we were going to attend. I was dispatched on a walk to the edge of the *iaz*. When I returned, they were ready to leave. We slogged back up the gritty embankment to the Lada. As we reached the highway, a second car slid to a stop behind Borya and Valentina's sedan. Borislav jumped out of the back seat. A thin, blond Russian-looking woman in her early twenties, long bangs drooping into her eyes, emerged from the front passenger seat.

Valentina stepped toward me, touching my arm. "*My* daughter," she said. Her tone implied a daughter who was hers alone, not

Borya's: a daughter from a previous marriage.

The daughter's husband was a large, dark young Russian named Oleg, very pudgy and trying to hide it by wearing his trousers absurdly high. His stomach bulged against the crotch of his slacks like the bellies of characters in illustrated editions of the novels of Charles Dickens. Both young people addressed me in Russian until Valentina stopped them. They seemed taken aback, almost offended, on learning I spoke Romanian. Valentina's daughter was hesitant about speaking Romanian, but once she overcame her shyness the words flowed in a natural patter and perfect accent. Odd holes in her vocabulary occasionally brought her up short in a kind of startled silence. To my surprise, her husband also managed a few Romanian phrases in a jokey, half-mocking way; he was the only Russian I ever heard utter a word of Romanian.

We set off in convoy into the countryside. I thought about the similarities between Valentina's and Dora's families. Both women had made second marriages to men significantly older than themselves. Both had a Russianized adult child, and a nine-year-old second child. Both second husbands were Romanian-speaking and comparatively nationalistic, though Senya was far more partisan than Borya. The contours were starker in Dora's family, but the pattern was the same: a return to the Romanian heritage calibrated in terms of small generational adjustments.

In the countryside little had changed. We drove thirty kilometres out of Chişinău, turned off the narrow highway, and wallowed over dusty roads riven by waist-deep potholes. Valentina's cousins—the children of the siblings of her Romanian mother—lived in a village spread over the lower reaches of a fertile hillside. Big farmhouses with sheds and animal cages tacked onto them like afterthoughts lined the streets of the village. The first farm we visited was in the centre of town. A large extended family occupied the house. Muscular men with unkempt hair and bedraggled black sideburns rolled out from under broken-down jalopies; little girls carried eggs into the house in their smocks; young men lugged buckets of water. Everyone spoke Romanian—everyone except old Uncle Nick from Australia. A tall, limber man in his seventies with curly white hair and a visage like a chipped rock face, he ambled out of the farmhouse. We greeted each other in English. Valentina and Borya greeted him in Russian. Serge and Borislav rushed off to watch a goat in a large cage being fed a meal of silage.

We ate lunch at a larger farm farther up the hillside, belonging to another of Valentina's cousins. Here the house gave onto the street and the sheds leaned up the slope behind. Goats, ducks, even a monstrous pig occupied makeshift cages. A little boy proudly showed me the pig, which raised its flattened, slurping snout in greeting. *"Este frumos, nu?"*

*"Foarte frumos!"* I replied. He was a very pretty pig!

Lunch was served outside at a long wooden table. I sat at the head, staring down the steep earthen driveway over the sprawling, half-forested village in the direction of layers of hills taller than those around Chişinău. Food seemed more abundant here than it was in the city, where Dora had to struggle to scrape together enough black bread, sausages, and wrinkled tomatoes to keep us all fed. Valentina's cousins trooped out of the house bearing bottles of Moldovan wine and plates of roast chicken, fried eggs, and milky cheese. There were fresh vegetables galore, including the cucumbers and tomatoes Valentina and Borya had brought. For dessert we ate a rich cake prepared by Valentina's daughter and drank a luminous light green mint tea.

Valentina's cousins couldn't revel in this sort of bounty every day. Even so, the undisturbed lushness of the countryside contrasted favourably with the deprivation and twisted cultural complexes of Chişinău. Here was a world deformed neither by Soviet commissars nor MTV. The village was a provincial place, backward in most respects, yet through this community traditional Romanian country life had continued to ramble along on its own course. Valentina's cousins knew who they were with a certainty that was denied to Valentina's children.

While the women cleared up, Borya invited me to accompany him on a walk up the steep hillside behind the animal sheds. We climbed through a grove to a clearing affording a wide view over hills radiant with a half-dozen shades of green as trees, bushes, grass, and gardens quailed before the wind.

"Brezhnev was the worst of them," Borya said into the silence. "The worst Soviet leader. When you went to the city with your family, you had to speak to each other in Russian or else you could be arrested as nationalist agitators. And the work was never here. I've worked all over Russia. I've been a logger in the taiga. I've fished as far north as Spitzbergen and Bear Island. I know Russian better than I know my own language. That's not right. But now Moldovan is the state language. As it should be. Now we've got our language back. Borislav is going to school in Moldovan."

That, he seemed to feel, was enough. Unlike Senya or Natasha, Borya didn't long for reunification with Romania. He didn't mention Lucinschi's new language law, and I could only assume he was much less disturbed by it than some of my students. The change would be easier to accept for those who defined their language as "Moldovan." To them Lucinschi's message was: "You've still got your language rights, but reunification is off the agenda." Only those, such as Natasha, who perceived Moldova as the lost or stolen half of Moldavia would be offended. But the majority of Romanian speakers—people like Valentina's cousins—remained in the countryside; they were poorly educated, depoliticized, and to some extent oblivious to what happened in the cities.

After lunch we changed into swimming trunks and drove in several packed cars to a very large, isolated *iaz* with wooded banks and a couple of pleasant natural beaches. Valentina had told me that the daughter of one of her cousins was judged an excellent student of French and would welcome the chance to speak to me in my other national language. The girl's brothers swarmed around me, urging me to talk to her. They ensured that we sat in the back seat of the same car on the drive to the *iaz*.

"Say something to Domnul Steve in French," the girl's mother urged her from the front seat. "Show him how well you speak the language of his country."

The girl, who appeared to be about sixteen, looked mortified. Her tanned face burned. She bowed her head until her lank, centre-parted brown hair drooped over her cheeks. Unsure whether addressing her in French would relieve her misery or accentuate it, I remained silent. The girl's brothers refused to let the issue drop. Their motives—possibly shared by the mother—became clear once we arrived at the *iaz*.

"Why don't you talk to her?" one of the boys asked, nudging me as we climbed out of the car.

I paused. Had I offended the girl by not speaking to her? I took a step toward her. She skittered away down the steep beach. The rest of the extended family splashed into the water; the girl clambered onto the trunk of a large tree that had fallen into the *iaz*. She sat above the fray, looking petrified.

Her brother pointed at her. "Look at that girl sitting on the tree. Don't you think she's beautiful? You could marry her if you wanted to."

So that was the plan—marry off his sister to the Westerner to establish a lifeline to the wealthy outside world. The boys' scheming was as naive as Andrei's fantasy of being healed by the Jacksons. Their plotting ruined their sister's afternoon. She spent the rest of the day shivering in terror on her fallen tree trunk.

I swam in the cold water, sat on the beach, ate, swam again, and talked with Borya and Valentina and their family. Eventually I sat next to old Uncle Nick. We spoke in English while the others regarded us with barely concealed fascination. Nick's English had a heavy Russian accent with a slight Australian overlay. He lived in Tasmania, where he had worked on the railways from his arrival at the end of World War II until his retirement in the mid-1980s. Married to a woman born in England, he had lost all his languages except for English and Russian. After graduating from the Romanian school system in the 1930s, Nick had pursued a career as a professional soccer player. I perked up at this news, telling him that my paternal grandfather had been a semiprofessional soccer player during the same period. Encouraged, Nick spoke of playing all over Europe. He had played in France and later been a member of a prestigious team in Vienna. He had spoken fluent German and good French and Russian in addition to his native Romanian. *Mitteleuropa*! I thought. In that polycultural world even athletes had been multilingual.

"The war destroyed everything," Nick said. Like so many people and cultures, his languages had been wiped out. His German and French vanished without a trace. Even his Romanian disappeared. An active Russian community centre in the town where he had settled in Tasmania rescued his Russian. The loss of his Romanian was a source of deep pain. "They say you never forget your first language. But it's not true."

Nick had come back to Moldova once before, in 1976, when his mother was terminally ill. The Soviet authorities had issued him a short-term visa on compassionate grounds. When he reached his mother's hospital bed, he found he couldn't speak to her. He had forgotten his Romanian and she, traumatized by Brezhnev's language policies, had suppressed her Russian. They sat opposite each other for a week without exchanging a word. Nick left the country a few days before his mother's death without having been able to say goodbye to her. This time he was determined to make amends. Once he had overcome his jet lag (he had just flown Hobart-Sydney-Tokyo-Moscow-Chişinău), he planned to start trying to recover his Romanian.

"Of course," he said, "the way these Moldovans speak, it's not like the Eminescu poems we memorized in school. People blame the way they speak on the Russians, but Moldovan's always been a difficult accent. It was like that before the Russians came." He looked around at Valentina's family staring back at us over towels and picnic leftovers, the wavelets of the *iaz* ebbing against the beach below us. "But

I'm hoping that by the end of my stay with these warm, hospitable people, I'll be able to speak my language again."

# 7

# CHIŞINĂU SNAPSHOTS

I gained my freedom like a Moldovan. Plumbing the depths of my confinement, I stumbled upon a fissure in my family's routines where I could move freely, then inexorably enlarged it. One afternoon as I finished teaching Serge and Borislav, Dora emerged from the sewing room accompanied by a sturdy woman in a blue print dress and two little girls. *"Mergem la izvor,"* Dora announced, inviting me to come along. She stepped into the kitchen and returned with a brace of large bottles.

We were going to a natural spring? Not quite believing her, I followed Dora out into the baking late-afternoon heat. We meandered downhill away from the high rises until we were walking along the lip of a steep, forested slope. A spring! Springs played an almost sacred role in Romanian, and particularly Moldavian, popular mythology. The earth's bounty in casting up jets of pure, gurgling water was portrayed with reverence by the novelist Mihail Sadoveanu. Later, in Romania, I would discover that thousands of Romanians fled the cities early on Saturday morning to spend their days off by rivers, lakes, and springs.

Dora turned off the sidewalk, leading the way downhill along a stone path laid across the reddish, needle-thick floor of the coniferous forest. A man walked uphill toward us with long strides, carrying on his shoulder in an almost ritualistic attitude a huge glass jar that lent the water inside a greenish crystalline tint. A moment later the path was blocked by a large stone shield. A spigot protruded from the back of the shield; water spilled out and splattered away down a rudimentary aqueduct. I stared uphill through the trees in the direction of the high rises clustered above us. *"Apa e buna?"*

"Yes, of course the water's good," Dora said. "It comes from deep in the earth."

I had found my cool, refreshing drink! At last I had a respite from rasping, headachey dehydration. It became my task to ensure that at all times two bottles of pure spring water sat cooling in the Lencuţas' fridge. The chore provided me with a pretext to leave the apartment alone. I discovered a second spring on the opposite side of the development at the edge of the highway leading to the open countryside of corn and sunflowers. Boxy Ladas and monstrous Kamaz trucks coughed to a halt, men and families climbing out to fill plastic buckets with clear, percolating water. My walks to the springs became longer and more wayward. *"Fac o plimbare la izvor"*—"I'm taking a walk to the spring"—became sufficient excuse to leave the apartment for hours. The *izvor* had liberated me. I could explore Chişinău on my own.

The U.S. Peace Corps volunteer slouched on the bench. A stocky, sincere, unworldly lad, he had been robbed at knife point his first night in Chişinău. But nothing was going to stop him doing good for folks in Moldova in as fair a way as he knew how. He showed me a page of Russian words he had copied out. Two Romanian speakers sat on either side of him, helping him to pronounce the words. One of the Romanian speakers, who spoke impressive English, had shared a drink the day before with Tony, the British colleague with whom I was walking along the street. He waved Tony over. We spoke for a few minutes to the Romanians and the Peace Corps volunteer. A large, bearded man came along the street, a notebook folded under his arm.

"This man's a writer," Tony's friend said. "He might be interested in talking to you."

"Does he speak English?" Tony asked. When his acquaintance shook his head, Tony said, "It's a bleeding shame being in a country and not speaking the language. I wish I could speak Russian!"

"You can't just speak Russian," the Romanian said. "Then everyone will think you're on the side of the Russians."

Tony turned toward me. Like virtually all of my colleagues, he had remained oblivious to Moldova's history and politics, dismissing as obscure ravings my attempts to offer some background. "So what you've been saying is true..."

Tony's acquaintance was apologizing to the writer. I heard him say in Romanian: "They don't understand anything. The English ones don't even know where they are."

The three Romanian speakers left, inviting the Peace Corps volunteer to accompany them. He bid me farewell. "These guys are gonna teach me Russian, and then they're gonna teach me Romanian. They've got two languages here, and I plan to treat them both equal."

I wished him good luck.

The Yankee dollar was everywhere. I glimpsed wads of U.S. dollars being passed from hand to hand in cafés on Ştefan Cel Mare Boulevard, dollar bills nestling among local currency when wallets were opened to pay for goods in shops. The disintegration of religion and ideology had opened the path for the dollar's ascent to deity. Entering middle-class apartments, I confronted enlarged photocopies of dollars mounted on living-room walls. Smaller photocopies winked from shop windows, coffee mugs, and car windshields. Like the icon of any new religion, the dollar had to be immaculate. Exchange booths rejected bills that were marred; the merest nick in the corner rendered a $100 bill worthless. It was useless to tell exchange-booth operators that rumpled bills were acceptable in the West. Dollars dated earlier than 1989—a magical year—were rejected. I once tried unsuccessfully to convert a $20 bill at four different exchange booths before extracting from one of the proprietors the information that my money was useless because it bore the date 1968, a year that was the antithesis of magic.

Determined to buy the Lencuţas a large bottled soft drink for dinner, I walked to the development's only bar. The cheap Formica tabletops reminded me of Ottawa Valley diners, the condensing cigarette smoke resembled a more acrid incarnation of the poisonous haze hanging over London parties, but the cramped quarters and weird assortment of Western music were inimitably East European: campy 1970s pop (the inevitable Boney M chanting "Ra! Ra! Rasputin!") and darkly morose underground bands succeeded each other indiscriminately. A large soft-drink bottle, costing more than a night's accommodation in an upcountry Moldovan inn, was an almost inexcusable extravagance. Yet I felt like blowing some money. Life in Chişinău was so austere that even I, repelled by recreational shopping in the West, found myself missing the opportunity to buy for the sake of buying.

There were three large soft-drink bottles for sale: one each of Pepsi, Fanta, and Bitter Lemon. The bottles stood on a shelf behind the counter, in the spot where in another country I might have expected to find a mounted set of antlers. I asked for the Bitter Lemon, paying with a ten-lei note. The woman behind the counter shortchanged me. Leaving her change on the counter, I said, "Two lei are missing."

She responded with a tangle of Russian. I repeated that I was short two lei. When that failed to produce results, I said, "I paid you ten lei, you've given me two lei change. You owe me two more lei."

She waved me away in Russian. Realizing she didn't understand Romanian, I tried to explain with a combination of words and gestures. Four men sitting at the table closest to the bar rocked in their chairs. One of them, very angry, harangued me in Russian. He thought I was bullying the woman for not speaking Romanian. He stubbed out his cigarette and got to his feet. Appealing to his companions, I explained the situation again. One of them understood. His shout calmed the woman behind the counter and brought his advancing buddy to a halt. The woman passed me the rest of my change. I folded my one-leu notes and stowed the bottle under my arm.

"You're from Romania, aren't you?" the one who had understood said as I walked past him toward the door.

It was inevitable he would think this: only someone from Romania would have the self-confidence to insist on being served in his own language. A Romanian-speaking Moldovan would have snapped obediently into Russian. "No," I said as I went out the door, "I'm from Chişinău."

During my afternoon siesta, I slipped on the headphones of my Walkman and dozed off to the sounds of Chişinău's lone popular-music station. The song lyrics were in English, the disc jockey's patter was in Romanian, but two-thirds of the voices that called in to request songs spoke Russian; the DJ would summarize the requests in Romanian. I suspected that some of the "Russian" callers were Romanian-speaking, yet nervous about using Romanian in a public situation. This nervousness saturated the city. It could be motivated by linguistic insecurities of very different types, ranging from the fear of making a grammatical error to a more raw, gut-wrenching fear inspired by memories of the Brezhnev years.

On the trolley buses the passenger standing closest to the punch machine inherited the job of punching everyone's tickets. One day, wedged against the gadget's tiny metal jaws, I accepted a woman's ticket, turned, and punched. The machine's toothless bite left no impression. I returned the ticket. *"Nu lucrează,"* I told the woman. "It's not working." The woman tensed like a culprit unmasked. She glanced around as though expecting the secret police to close in. A moment later she pushed away into a safer pocket of the crowd. The language of trolley-bus etiquette remained a mystery to me. The small, stocky ticket collectors in worn grey smocks who elbowed their way through the massed passengers on the express buses spoke only Russian. Yet the accepted phrases for inquiring whether the person beside you was getting off at the next stop were Romanian. *"Coborîți?"* you would ask. Your neighbour, if planning to descend, would reply: *"Cobor."* Here, somehow, a Romanian phrase had become institutionalized; all other trolley-bus inquiries were made in Russian.

The higher realms of human activity—government, administration, culture—remained dominated by Russian language and taste. When I took letters to the post office, where all the signs and notices were in Romanian, the clerks proved unable to read the Latin alphabet. They asked me to tell them each letter's country of destination so they could affix the correct postage. Sometimes they scrawled the country's name in Russian at the bottom of the envelope. Among the city's many flimsy newspapers, I finally found one I liked: a brash, youthful weekly called *Generația* that mingled flamboyant muckraking, international celebrity gossip, translations of opinion essays from foreign newspapers, and doses of Romanian-language nationalism that crossed the spectrum from the thoughtful to the disconcertingly intolerant. Entering the living room to find me reading *Generația*, Dora asked, "Can you read that?"

"It's not too difficult," I said, assuming she was referring to the vocabulary.

She shook her head. "I can't read that alphabet. I find Cyrillic easier." She disappeared into the bedroom and returned with the book from her bedside table. "I usually read crime novels, but now I'm reading this." Inspecting the fat volume she passed me, I worked out that it was a Russian translation of Theodore Dreiser's *An American Tragedy*, the single most popular piece of Western literature in the former Soviet Union. Dora's life was permeated not only by the Russian language, but by Russian preferences. Her situation wasn't unique: everyone was affected by the confusion of having lost a culture. Even defiantly unassimilated Natasha knew less than she wished about Romanian literature.

Pondering this, I turned the page of *Generaţia* and gaped as I discovered a translation of an article by Mr. Sterne, my undergraduate international relations professor. As I read, memories rushed back of classes with Mr. Sterne at the U.S. liberal arts college where I had completed my B.A. Mr. Sterne, who was rumoured to have been driven out of Harvard after a dispute with Henry Kissinger, had lectured on the trot, staring straight ahead as he cut back and forth before the blackboard. His voice dipped and peaked in a hacking chant that expelled every tenth or twelfth word as a yell. The knowledge we gleaned from him was uncomfortable: "And, of course, the Nazis in Ge*rrr*many were supported by people like *yourselves*!"

I owed one of the kernels of my obsession with cultural politics to Mr. Sterne. Lecturing on the rise of the transnational corporation in the aftermath of World War II, Mr. Sterne had turned on the class like a prosecutor. "Transnational corporations adapt to countries, then *change* them. And who are the people you adapt to most easily?"

"People like yourselves?" a tentative voice said.

"Yes, Ms. Javitz. And in 1945, for the United States of America, who was *that*?"

"Western Europe," a bearded man stated with deep-voiced confidence.

"Germany? Italy?" Mr. Sterne said. "In 1945 how much did the United States share with Germany or *Italy*, Mr. O'Reilly?"

"England," the bearded man said.

"Wrong!" Mr. Sterne cried. "Who is most like *us*? What is the easiest environment for U.S. corporations to enter and control in the years after 1945?"

Voices volleyed from the corners of the room, repeating the same names: England, Western Europe, France and, in a tone of desperation, Iceland.

"You're missing the obvious." Mr. Sterne resumed his blind pacing, then stopped. "Mr. Henighan knows. Don't you, Mr. Henighan?"

"They started in Canada," I said.

"That's right," Mr. Sterne said. "*Canada!*"

As I had discovered to be customary when this word was uttered in a U.S. college classroom, a sprinkle of snickers was audible. Undeterred, Mr. Sterne continued to pace, detailing the surrender of national enterprise in Canada before the encroachment of transnational corporations during the 1950s and 1960s. "Canada today," he concluded, "has a *branch-plant* economy. Isn't that right, Mr. Henighan?"

"Y-yes, Mr. Sterne," I stammered. "Though the social and cultural effects of that are offset by the fact that our state sector is more activist than yours."

"You can mitigate the effects," Mr. Sterne said, "but you can't eliminate the structure. And once the structure had been established in *Canada*, transnational corporations moved on to environments which were *harder* to adapt to..."

The prelude to my thinking about globalization had taken place in Mr. Sterne's lectures about the harbinger role Canada had played during the spread of transnational corporations in the 1950s and 1960s. Discovering an article by my former professor in a newspaper in faraway Moldova, in an era when the Canadian branch-plant economy had been obliterated by free trade, felt both incongruous and serendipitous.

Reading the article, I discovered that in the decade since I had studied with him, Mr. Sterne's analysis had evolved. In the world that had emerged from the decay of the Soviet Union and the winding down of superpower rivalry, Mr. Sterne argued, political power would be projected through the ability to impose your culture on others. I looked up from the newspaper. Dora sat in the bedroom reading *An American Tragedy* in Russian; Andrei, in the sewing room, was watching MTV, delivering U.S. songs via a Russian network. Once again Mr. Sterne seemed to have a point.

The Museum of Moldovan History was a building of Latinate grandeur fronted by a broad white facade, wide front steps, and a vast, echoing entrance hall. The statue at the gate depicted Romulus and Remus being suckled by a she-wolf. The assertion was unmistakable: Moldovans were Romanians and Romanian history began with the mythological foundation of Rome by the two boys raised by a wolf.

The large, sparsely stocked display rooms on the second floor strained to confirm this vision. Yet the mosaic cracked constantly. Climbing the marble staircase, I realized I was the museum's only visitor. Each room or corridor was attended by four or five women in drab smocks who sat murmuring to one another in the gloom. As I entered, they turned on the lights; as soon as I had passed, the lights were extinguished and those of the next room illuminated. The displays betrayed an improvised, even slapdash air, as though all the extant evidence corroborating Moldova's Romanian character had been hastily dragged together. Archaeological fragments from ancient Dacia lay next to World War I–era diplomas from Romanian-language Chişinău secondary schools. I examined venerable Latin-alphabet typewriters, watches, framed scraps of newspapers. There was even a letter from Stephen the Great. But, leaning forward, I saw that I couldn't read it: Stephen had written in the Cyrillic alphabet!

The realization that the supreme defender of Moldavian sovereignty had written in Cyrillic brought me to a stunned halt. The fact was hardly surprising: throughout Central and Eastern Europe the alphabet had come from the church. Orthodox cultures, such as the Serbs, Bulgarians, Russians, and Ukrainians, wrote in Cyrillic; Roman Catholic cultures, such as the Poles, Czechs, Hungarians, and Croats, used the Latin alphabet. Modern Romanians are an anomaly in that they are Orthodox but write in the Latin alphabet (the same phenomenon occurs in reverse in western Ukraine, where a predominantly Catholic population uses the Cyrillic alphabet). So much was said in contemporary Moldova about Stephen the Great's defence of Christian Moldavia against "the godless east"—meaning the Muslim Turks, but referring covertly to Soviet communism—that it was easy to forget that the Christianity Stephen was defending had been of the Orthodox variety, the same Christianity professed by many of the "godless" Russians who had brought the Soviet Empire to Moldova.

I stopped for a long time in front of Stephen the Great's letter. The thick-stroked arabesques of Stephen's quill made me realize that the loss of history so frequently decried by Romanian-speaking Moldovans was a lethal double-edged sword. It was true that Moldovans educated in the Cyrillic alphabet couldn't read classical or contemporary Romanian literature or history. But citizens of modern Romania, it suddenly occurred to me, couldn't read *their* literature prior to the late eighteenth century when the pan-Latin movement based in Transylvania, deciding that the "racial" links with the Latin world would take precedence over the religious connections to Byzantium, threw out the Cyrillic curlicues and began to rewrite the language in Latin script, cramming their pages with French loan words and resuscitated Latin neologisms.

Romanian-speaking Moldovans, ironically, had access to a deeper history of Romanian-language culture than did Romanian citizens: denied the training to read the poems of Eminescu or the novels of

Sadoveanu, they could nevertheless scrutinize the treaties and theological discourses of the sixteenth to the eighteenth centuries. For people in Romania, raised with the Latin alphabet, the past began in the 1830s. The tortured ambiguity expressed by many Moldovans thrummed with a new resonance. It wasn't merely that these people had been colonized by the Soviet Empire; their education in the Cyrillic alphabet had infected them with a traitorous awareness that despite the shrieking pan-Latinism of Ceauşescu's mad final years, despite statues of Romulus and Remus, the roots of Romanian written culture lay in the Slavic-dominated Orthodox church. The "return to Rome" in the late eighteenth and early nineteenth centuries had repudiated a thousand-year-old tradition.

This rupture's preliminary spasms appeared in a later display: a book of eighteenth-century Romanian poetry written in an uneasily modified Cyrillic script, its spidery lines interrupted by the presence of the letter *i*—which doesn't exist in the standard Cyrillic alphabet (though it appears in the Ukrainian and Serbian variants)—and the addition of Latinate diacritical marks. Where all this was leading became evident in the largest of the display rooms, devoted to a panoramic exhibition of woodcuts by an artist named Victor Zâmbarea. The woodcuts depicted the deportation to Siberia of the Moldovan middle class in 1949. They were startlingly vivid. Stunned people were rounded up and herded into trains. Bowed figures waded through deep snow, guard dogs worrying at their heels. Miserable-looking deportees chopped wood outside snowbound huts. I thought about Dora's preference for the Cyrillic alphabet and Russian taste, wondering how different her associations might have been had her vanished middle-class compatriots remained in Moldova.

A team of assistants worked full-time to keep us in the country. Brisk men spent their days typing up forms and visiting government offices to secure and extend working visas; when problems arose between teachers and families, two sympathetic young women arrived to translate and mediate. Paula, an attractive woman of about twenty, her long, loose, thick brown hair a shade darker than her deeply tanned face and arms, was the assistant we came to know best. She had met our train in Lvov and travelled to Chişinău with us. She loved to idle in the office and never refused an invitation to go out for a beer. As a result of this assiduous socializing, she spoke superbly fluid English with a shy softness of voice. Every time I met her Paula was wearing the same shin-length, copper-coloured dress. Financially, though, she seemed to be doing better than most Moldovans. In addition to her contract as an assistant to the English teachers, she worked for a Western embassy, translating from Russian and Ukrainian into English. She said that her family was of Ukrainian ancestry, though her sloe-eyed, dark-skinned, almost Central Asian look reminded me of no Ukrainian I had met. Near the end of my stay in Chişinău I ran into Paula in Ştefan Cel Mare Park. She was standing with two of the teachers. All three of them looked upset. Afraid I had barged in on an emotional moment, I said nothing.

"Paula has to leave Moldova," one of the teachers said.

"Why?" I asked.

"My father says there's no future here." Paula's shyness dissolved in a burst of vehemence. "No future for people like us. For people who don't speak Moldovan."

We were standing in a grove of linden trees. Over Paula's shoulder, along the paved paths, unemployed young men sat reading on park benches. Statues of Romanian poets watched over them. "You could always learn Mold...Romanian," I said. "You've learned English."

"But nobody cares how you speak English. I will never speak Moldovan like a Moldovan. Anyway, my father has made up his mind. We're moving to Germany."

"Germany?"

"Yes, after all the *work* I have done to learn English now I must start a new language. A hard language. My father says he doesn't want to leave Europe. I said, 'Why can't we go to England then?' But there is a business he can join in Germany. He knows we can get visas..." She shook her head and shrugged, her glossy hair sliding on her shoulders.

A year and a half later a friend from Berlin came to visit me in England. Sharing a fascination with Central and Eastern Europe, we traded anecdotes about our respective travels. As I paused to catch my breath, my friend said, "I met a Moldovan girl once. In Berlin."

"Where?"

"At the Goethe Institute," she said. "I went to ask about teaching. They were doing renovations and you had to go in a door at the side. This girl asked me where the entrance was. I asked her where she was from and she said Moldova. I told her I had a friend who had taught English in Moldova and she said she used to work with English tea—"

"Paula! It must have been Paula!"

"For someone who had been in Berlin only a few weeks," my friend said, "her German was *very* good."

Chişinău received four television stations in two languages: two Russian stations from Moscow; Moldovan television, which alternated between Romanian and Russian; and, as a recent addition, TVR1 from Bucharest. The only Moldovan program anyone in the Lencuţa family watched was *Mesager*, the nightly newscast. For entertainment they turned to Moscow. MTV was transmitted via Moscow, as was an endless stream of Third World B-movies, with Indian and Mexican films predominating. Russian television neither subtitled nor dubbed foreign films; rather, the dialogue was muted and a deadpan Russian voice-over competed with the original soundtrack: *Where is he? He's in the other room. Oh, my God, he's dead. Call the police...* On and on the voice went, no squeak of expression enlivening its tombstone delivery. I understood none of it; when no one else was home, I would switch to TVR1 to watch Romanian plays, documentaries, popular singers, and news.

I had been watching TVR1 for nearly three weeks when I saw Romanian President Iliescu for the first time. The contrast with Moldovan television was conspicuous. Every night *Mesager* would open with the words: "Today the president of the Republic of Moldova, Mr. Mircea Snegur..." Each night's news led with a press-release version of Snegur's activities. His jowly face expressionless, Snegur visited schools, inspected cooperatives, greeted visiting Russian officials. Interviews with Snegur's ministers were conducted with grovelling obsequiousness. I later read a report by a U.S. think tank that was devastatingly critical of the Romanian TVR1's pro-government bias, but viewed from Chişinău, TVR1 was a throbbing beehive of democratic debate.

Only once did I see Moldovan television fleetingly acknowledge the existence of opposition to government policy. On the day the Parliament ratified Petru Lucinschi's law changing the country's official language from Romanian to "Moldovan," Senya and I watched the camera panning the curved tiers of the small legislature. Once the majority Democratic Agrarian Party had pushed the bill through, prominent Agrarians cooed to an acquiescent interviewer that they had fulfilled the will of the people, guaranteeing prosperity and social peace. After receiving a number of these homilies to "tolerance," the journalist announced we would hear the opinions of the opposition. The camera focused on a furious, bearded man, his body stiff with intransigence. He began to speak rapidly: "This is an oppressive, unjust law! We—"

The camera swung away. The opposition member had been allowed to utter fewer than ten words on air. Nothing in the remainder of the broadcast hinted that the new language law had been greeted with less than universal acclaim.

Senya watched the coverage in silence, his small body braced. He ignored my request to know his opinion. Perhaps, for the moment, silence was his only option. I remembered Theresa's advice to Natasha that this might be a time to say nothing. But Senya's silence was no strategic retreat: he looked crushed.

He fell equally silent on the night of General Lebed's press conference. I had never seen an event like this. Senya and I were sitting in the living room, flipping distractedly between TVR1 and the Moldovan channel as we waited for *Mesager*. Without warning a man in a funereal suit appeared on the Moldovan network to tell us in a pious voice that regular programming would be suspended because General Lebed, the Russian military commander in the Slavic breakaway region of Trans-Dniestria, wished to give a press conference. A holding pattern froze the screen, yielding a few minutes later to a shot of what looked like a schoolroom. The brawny, vigorous-looking Lebed, resembling a Central American guerrilla leader in his combat fatigues, sat behind a desk on a raised platform at the front of the room. Twenty or thirty awkwardly upright men in suits occupied the wooden benches below: obedient pupils awaiting a lesson. Lebed spoke in Russian. No translation or subtitles were offered. No questions were solicited.

The term *press conference* was a misnomer for this event; even *briefing* failed to capture the growling menace of Lebed's harangue. He spoke without notes for a half hour. His voice sounded less sonorous and high-pitched than most Russian voices; the camera caught his huge hands pawing the air in front of his chest. Whenever he needed to gather his thoughts, Lebed lapsed into silence, supremely confident that everyone in the room—everyone in the country—would remain attentive until he was ready to resume. The camera focused on the general from the side, transmitting most of the press conference through a close-up, low-angle shot of his pugnacious jaw and surprisingly youthful face. Once Lebed was in full snarling flight, the camera risked jerky panning shots of the crowd of solemn men in suits wedged into children's benches. As the view widened, another man appeared, sitting next to Lebed on the long, raised desk: a trim, crew-cut, mostly bald individual in uniform. I recognized his face from photographs.

"Bergman!" Senya snorted.

Colonel Michial Bergman was in charge of the daily running of the city of Tiraspol. An elusive political gamesman, he sometimes seemed to be working with Lebed and at other times took positions implicitly critical of the general. To what extent these shifting allegiances were orchestrated for public consumption was anyone's guess; the two men's appearance together at the press conference sent a signal that for the moment they were on the same side. Bergman had denounced the Trans-Dniestrian government's corruption and its conversion of Tiraspol into a haven for gunrunners and criminals from all over Eastern Europe and Eurasia.

"Everything that is being produced here is being taken out," Bergman had told a foreign researcher. "The money is stored in foreign banks, witnesses are killed, deputies frightened, and the ministers who bear responsibility for law and order are criminals themselves." During one of his crackdowns on the Tiraspol Mafia, Bergman had arrested fifteen hundred people in one week, only to have them all released by the Trans-Dniestrian prosecutor-general. Anti-Semitic Russian nationalist groups (many of whom worshipped Lebed) had vowed to assassinate Bergman, who was of Jewish ancestry. Bergman's survival—both professionally and personally—was an impressive feat.

As Bergman stooped demurely in the background, Lebed ranted. When the press conference ended, I looked to Senya for his reaction. He turned off the television. After a long, pained silence, he said, "This business of Trans-Dniestria tears the soul."

He disappeared into the bedroom.

My Chişinău snapshots couldn't give me the full picture. The city was incomplete without its grim twin, Tiraspol. What happened there, I realized, sculpted much of what happened here. I had no choice: I must visit Tiraspol.

# 8

# LEBED'S KINGDOM

I had travelled through Trans-Dniestria once before.

In mid-afternoon, on the train from Lvov to Chişinău, we had crossed the border out of Ukraine. Grim Ukrainian officials collected some of the rotting scraps of grey paper we had filled in on the Polish border; they stamped us out of the country. But no Moldovan officials arrived to interrogate or greet us. We had left one country without entering another. The train lumbered into limbo.

That administrative limbo had been the Trans-Dniestrian Republic.

Trans-Dniestria is a thin, jagged-edged slice of land between the Dniester River and the Ukrainian border. This is the strip of Ukraine with which Bessarabia was combined in 1940 to create the Moldavian Soviet Socialist Republic. The region is about forty percent Romanian-speaking; the Slavic majority is divided between Ukrainians and Russians, including a substantial Jewish minority. Since Moldova acquired the land only in 1940, and then under Soviet fiat, Chişinău's claim to the territory has been contested. The government contends that the Republic of Moldova consists of all of the Moldavian Soviet Socialist Republic, not merely historical Bessarabia; a strong feeling of obligation persists toward Romanians living beyond the

Dniester River. This feeling was strengthened by the authoritarian pan-Slavism that came to power in Tiraspol after Moldova's independence declaration sparked a Trans-Dniestrian declaration of secession.

When Chişinău sought to enforce its claim to Trans-Dniestria, General Lebed ordered the Russian Fourteenth Army to intervene on the side of the separatists. A brief, brutal war in May and June 1992 confirmed the creation of an unrecognized but unconquerable Slavic homeland in Trans-Dniestria. As a result of this war and some of the earlier clashes that set the stage for full-scale conflict, more than a thousand people were killed and over one hundred and thirty thousand became refugees. Brandishing the threat of invasion, Lebed forced the government in Chişinău to extend "temporary special status" to the new "republic." Since that concession, the Moldovan military, police force, judges, and customs and immigration officials had been expelled from the region.

One of the results of this stalemate was that Moldova had no effective eastern border. The Trans-Dniestrian authorities, denying Moldova's claim to the territory, refused to allow Moldovan customs and immigration officials to set up shop on the Ukrainian border. The Moldovan government, not wishing to concede de facto recognition of Trans-Dniestrian autonomy, refused to establish a border post on the Dniester River, where effective Moldovan authority began. Trucks and trains arriving from Ukraine sailed into the country unmonitored and occasionally undocumented. By contrast the border with Romania—as I would discover to my chagrin—was fiercely policed. This openness to the east (while maintaining barricades to the west) was one of the more salient ways in which the contours of the Soviet Union were perpetuated.

When we first arrived in Chişinău, climbing off the train far down the platform, a small moustached man named Igor appeared carrying a colourful plastic bag. We were ordered to toss our passports into Igor's bag. Two weeks later the passports came back stamped with Moldovan working visas in bright red Romanian lettering. The country without a border nevertheless had its own visas and stamps. What it didn't have was sovereignty over its territory.

In 1975 Marin Preda, the dominant Romanian novelist of the post-1945 era, published an epic novel called *Delirul* (*The Frenzy*), set during the years leading up to Romania's entry into World War II. Romanian censorship butchered the novel, excising many key scenes—notably Preda's dramatizations of the married life of Joseph Stalin—and insisting on the addition of a chapter praising the Romanian dictator Nicolae Ceauşescu. Disheartened, Preda complied, but the harassment persuaded him to abandon the novel's sequel, in which he had planned to dramatize the events of World War II. In 1991, when both Ceauşescu and Preda were dead (the latter possibly murdered by the former's secret police), *Delirul* was republished in an uncensored edition. The novel offers intriguing insights into the 1930s; it is Olivia Manning's *Balkan Trilogy* rewritten by an insider. Among other attributes, *Delirul* is one of the very few works by a Romanian Gentile to acknowledge the genocide of much of Romania's Jewish population, describing the persecution of Jews in the countryside in brutally frank prose. Preda's denunciatory portrait of General Antonescu, Romania's wartime fascist leader, remains controversial. During the novel's closing chapters, the protagonist, Paul Ştefan, is sent as a war correspondent to Bessarabia, where Romanian troops are pushing toward the Dniester River.

The Romanian army's recapturing of Trans-Dniestria and its conquest of southern Russia remains a vivid memory to Romanians and Moldovans. To this day extreme Romanian nationalists display maps on which Odessa appears within Romania's borders. But even the majority of Romanians who were satisfied with the more modest boundaries of the "Greater Romania" of the interwar years felt that Trans-Dniestria was an integral part of their country, a missing sliver. Stalin, ironically, confirmed the Romanian nationalist credo that Moldavia and Trans-Dniestria were a single entity when he combined them to create the Moldavian Soviet Socialist Republic.

In *Delirul* the Romanian commander Radu Ruşeţeanu evinces no doubts about the justice of conquering Trans-Dniestria. His orders from General Antonescu to advance on Odessa and continue fighting "to the final victory," though, tip him into a moral crisis. He doesn't wish to enter another country's history books as an invader: "that is not our destiny." Through Ruşeţeanu, Preda argues that Romanian nationalism's sometimes boundless territorial ambitions must recognize certain limits, based on Romanians' own historical experience of having suffered conquest. Territorial revindications must be tempered by moral precepts. Ruşeţeanu's response to Antonescu's command to continue until "the final victory" is to ask: "And if that victory doesn't come? A people such as ours has to ask itself these questions. In the end even Stephen the Great came to terms with the Turks, once he had repelled them from Moldavian soil."

Against his own judgement, Ruşeţeanu follows orders and drives forward to Odessa. He vanquishes the Soviet army, but the city's outraged citizens take their revenge by blowing him up in his headquarters. Paul Ştefan, the novel's hero, escapes to Bucharest only to discover that his ferociously impartial dispatches from the front have been mutilated by editors who have inflated his prose with the wooden language of Romanian nationalism, inserting "bombastic propositions, mystical expressions about the cross and the race, martyrs and reliquaries, the graves of the ancestors, history and eternity..."

It would be hard to imagine a Romanian writer more opposed to the quasi-mystical nationalist dementia inspired by the notion of "Greater Romania" than Preda. Yet even Preda is firm about Trans-Dniestria: it is Romanian. General Lebed was equally firm. "The Dniester area is the key to the Balkans," he told a reporter. "If Russia withdraws from this little piece of land, it will lose the key and its influence in that region." In addition to his strategic concerns, Lebed evoked moral principle: the enclave's Slavs, accounting for more than fifty-four percent of its six hundred thousand people, couldn't be abandoned. Lebed's moral principle collided with that of

Preda (and Senya and nearly all other speakers of Romanian). Two claims, both based on sound morality, that contradicted each other: Sophocles would have revelled in the dilemma. For the residents of Trans-Dniestria—particularly the forty percent of the population that was Romanian-speaking—the collision of moralities promised years of hardship.

"Tiraspol?" Senya had said when I told him of my outing. "Why do you want to go there? It's a little town!" Now I found myself in the Tiraspol train station with eleven colleagues: twelve university-educated people in our twenties and thirties and not a single one of us capable of deciphering the Cyrillic schedules posted on the wall. My mention of my plans to the group of English teachers who gathered every afternoon on the bench behind the statue of Stephen the Great had elicited an unexpectedly eager response. I had hoped to persuade two or three people to accompany me, not a regiment.

Military metaphors came to mind naturally here: Tiraspol was a garrison. Trains arriving from Chişinău—two hours' journey on the slumberous railway line—rolled into the face of a tank whose barrel was aimed at the incoming rolling stock. The wall of the small square outside the station was blemished by a large plaque from whose embossed surface thrust the profile of V. I. Lenin. I had expected our excursion to Tiraspol to be a sort of day trip to Russia; it was more like a voyage back in time to the Soviet Union. Lenin was every-where. The Moldovan leu was worthless. We had to change U.S. dollars into "Trans-Dniester roubles": Russian roubles, Lenin resplendent on the front of each note, with a small sticker of General Suvarov plastered in the corner to certify them as Trans-Dniestrian currency. Trans-Dniestria had adopted Suvarov, an eighteenth-century Russian general who slaughtered Romanians with staggering bloodthirstiness, as its founding inspiration. In 1790 Suvarov had razed the Moldavian city of Ismail, massacring its inhabitants. The general's statue stood guard over the Dniester River. The message to Chişinău could hardly have been clearer. The only imaginable equivalent to Trans-Dniestria's choice of Suvarov as its emblem would be for banknotes featuring portraits of Adolf Hitler to circulate in the Gaza Strip.

The cramped train station jostled with uniformed members of the Dniester Guard wearing the Russian colours on their shoulder flashes. Two Guard trucks were parked in the square outside. We walked toward the centre of town, dispersing into small groups. The day was less oppressive than most days that summer, but I felt suffocated. I had known, of course, that the Latin alphabet had been outlawed in Trans-Dniestria and the city's only Romanian-language school closed. In the countryside, where most Romanian speakers lived, Romanian schools remained open but the language had to be written in the Cyrillic alphabet. Trans-Dniestria, which had belonged to the Soviet Union since 1917, had been the proving ground for the language policies imposed on Bessarabia after World War II. In 1924 the Soviets mandated that the region's Romanian speakers write their language in the Cyrillic alphabet. The attempt to manufacture a Russified Romanian dialect under the rubric of "Moldovan," and to assert that this dialect and Romanian were mutually incomprehensible, had begun in Tiraspol.

None of this information prepared me for the shock of entering a city in what was, after all, Moldovan territory, from which the Latin alphabet had been expunged. The suppression of Latin influences was cultural as well as alphabetical: walking along the broad, bare streets of the centre of Tiraspol, I longed for the showy, languid warmth of Chișinău. Tiraspol had no street life, no flare or flamboyance. I felt deprived. People plodded about their business. There was no loitering, no sidewalk stalls, no hucksterism or gossip; the city lived for its rancour.

Twice in two blocks young men stepped into the glaring sunlight and belted out hassling snarls at me and the two colleagues with whom I was walking. Hungry, I turned into a bakery, joining a mute lineup for bread. When I reached the head of the queue, I mimicked the request I had heard people in front of me uttering. I was greeted with a long, hard stare. After a moment's pause, during which no one in the bakery breathed, I was passed a loaf of bread. I handed over a note bearing the images of Lenin and Suvarov, pocketed the change I was offered, and escaped with my loaf. Bread seemed to be the only food for sale in Tiraspol. The Trans-Dniester rouble, which was faring poorly, was due to be replaced in a few months' time by a Trans-Dniester coupon, on which Lenin's face would yield to that of Suvarov. But the genocidal general seemed destined to lose the economic battle. Despite infusions of fraternal Slavic aid from Moscow, Trans-Dniestria's fanatical isolationism had proved nearly suicidal. Chişinău's austerity looked like abundance by comparison with the starkness of life in Tiraspol.

Most of the population appeared to spend weekend afternoons at the scrubby beaches along the Dniester River. We crossed a bridge, descending to the riverbank. Families waded in the stagnant water; a muted reflection of Chişinău's festiveness became discernible. Returning across the bridge, I met two of the women in our group. They had just encountered the Dniester Guard. "They asked to see our passports," Alice, a Nordic-looking woman with short blond hair and a prim South-of-England accent, said. "They told us to get into the back of their van while they looked at them."

"What did you do?" I asked.

"We gave them our passports, but I jolly well wasn't going to get into their van. They looked at our passports for *ages*. They couldn't make head or tail of them, of course. They tried to tell us our passports were illegal because they weren't written in Russian. It was a good half hour before they let us go."

Five of us walked together toward the Trans-Dniestrian Supreme Soviet. A faceless building of bureaucratic functionalism, the Supreme Soviet acquired a glowering authority from its position overlooking the river. In front of the building, striding toward its doors, was a gigantic statue of Lenin. Counting its podium, the statue towered three stories high. Across the street, between the Supreme

Soviet and the Dniester River, stretched the concrete tiers of a vast memorial ground. A tank mounted on a platform dominated the memorial area, which seemed to have been built to commemorate the dead of World War II. But as I approached the heat of the eternal flame and bent over the photographs mounted on the small symmetrical tombs, I saw from the inscriptions that all the faces belonged to Slavic men killed in the 1992 civil war against Chişinău. The inscribed dates of birth and death revealed that all but one of the men had died in their late teens or early twenties. The exception, an officer in his forties, was commemorated by a stern grey photograph in full uniform. The photographs were surrounded by bunches of fresh flowers.

I pulled my camera out of my pocket and, discreetly as I could, photographed the tank and the memorial. Before I could take photographs of the Supreme Soviet, the Lenin statue, or the tombs, a group of young men at the edge of the memorial ground began to walk toward us. One of them waved us away from the tombs. We didn't move. They kept coming.

I glanced at my colleagues. Deciding we had all had enough trouble for one day, we turned and walked back down the riverbank.

A short dark man walking in front of us turned around at the sound of our English. He called out to us in broken English with a strong French accent. "How long have you been here?" I asked him in French.

"Almost a week. I am staying with exquisitely kind people. They do not have much food, but they are very kind." Standing against the stone parapet, the shallow gorge falling away behind him to the beaches on the opposite bank, he puffed out his chest. "I am a Jehovah's Witness. I met a marvellous family at a Jehovah's Witness conference in Kiev and they invited me to come home with them." He glanced out over the river. "Russia's pretty, isn't it?"

"You think this is Russia?"

He frowned. Then, as if drawing to mind a remote memory, he said, "*Ah, oui.* There is some sort of political problem, *n'est-ce pas?*

But I don't understand such things. I don't think they are very important. Would you like—"

I interrupted him. "Have you met other foreigners in Tiraspol?"

Once again he puffed out his chest. "I believe I am the only one. Would you like to come home with me for a few minutes? I can give you some very good literature. It's in French, so you'll be able to read it. About our faith—"

Another creed! I glanced at the heroic features of General Suvarov surging from the memorial towering above us. Turning to my colleagues, I said, "I think it's time to go back to Chişinău."

# 9

# A LONG DRUNK

The Lencuţas' family life began to deteriorate the day Dora left on vacation. I should have seen it coming. The week preceding Dora's departure Andrei became increasingly tense. His job was going badly: the televisions in the sewing room weren't selling and his boss was growing impatient. He began to drink. In his boozy agitation he developed an obsession with my Walkman and hounded me to sell it to him. Andrei was willing to indebt himself for two years to buy the Walkman at its Western price. I was tempted to donate it to him when I left the country, but a mixture of noble and ignoble motives persuaded me this was the wrong course of action. Andrei persisted in referring to my Walkman as the "Player," no matter how many times I told him English-speaking people wouldn't call it that. "Steve! Player!" he would say in the bossy way he often spoke to me, as though I were too dim to grasp basic facts. *"Vreau să ascult!"*

I couldn't resist his entreaties. He had so little; he might never have a Walkman of his own. He listened to the radio with the volume cranked up so high that the music being pumped into his ears tingled through the adjoining rooms. He rang up friends and invited them around to see the Walkman. Young men in track suits trooped into the apartment to discuss how the gadget compared with the Walkmans owned by nouveau riche Russians of their acquaintance.

"*Te rog,*" I begged him as I left for work. "Don't listen to the Walkman all day. It's bad for your ears and it's bad for the batteries."

When I came home, the batteries were dead. There was no point in getting angry. I had brought a spare pair from England, anticipating—correctly—that batteries would be virtually unobtainable in Moldova. In the future, I decided, I would ration Andrei's Walkman listening.

Teaching the little dictators, then the little boys, had exhausted me. After supper I lay on the living-room couch to doze, listening to the radio at low volume on fresh batteries.

Half an hour later the earphones were yanked from my head. Andrei absconded with the Walkman and presented it to two visiting friends. He was drunk. They were speaking Russian, but I could see that the other two weren't taking him seriously. They examined the Walkman, made a few comments, then escaped. I roamed around the apartment; Dora, Senya, and Serge had vanished. Andrei seemed pained by their absence. "Steve," he said, treading the living-room carpet with burly deliberation, "you've got to help me bring the Jacksons here."

"Andrei!" I was close to losing my temper. His delusions made me furious: furious with the way satellite television fed these illusions to people who had been stripped of their cultural defences and furious with Andrei for being among the vulnerable.

"There is a fight in a family... The Jacksons can come and make it better."

"You think the Jacksons are a happy family?" I asked.

"We need money. You have to get Pepsi to give money. You have to talk to them, Steve. You can bring Pepsi here. You can tell them in English how much money we'll all make from this—"

"Andrei, this is a stupid idea. I'm not going to talk about it anymore!"

He stalked off to his room. I sat on the purple couch, breathing heavily. Andrei returned carrying a sheaf of letters and photographs. He sat next to me on the couch, dropping letters between us. "Steve," he said, looking straight ahead, not meeting my eyes, "I'm afraid. I'm afraid that if I don't make money soon I'm going to lose my girl."

I was surprised. I hadn't observed a girlfriend in Andrei's life, though various young women had slipped into the apartment for innocently flirtatious visits at moments when Dora and Senya were absent. I recalled Dora telling me that at the age of seventeen Andrei had announced he was going to marry a Russian girl. "But we stopped it," Dora had said. "We told him he had to be able to buy his own apartment first." This was the tragedy of young people in Moldova: no sex without marriage, no marriage without an apartment, no apartment without a steady job. But nobody under the age of thirty-five had a job. Young adults slept in their parents' living rooms, watched MTV, drank away their frustrations, made occasional lurching forays into "business." Yet the cultural preference for early marriages remained. To be twenty-five and unmarried was scandalous, but no parent wanted a grown child sleeping in the living room with a spouse (and, within a few months, a baby). This might work in the countryside, but Chişinău apartments couldn't accommodate multi-generational families. The contradiction between the demands of culture and the constraints enforced by economics was tearing up the lives of Andrei's generation.

Andrei showed me photographs of the girl he had wanted to marry: a Russian Jew he had met in Moscow. She looked well groomed and plumply pretty. "I'm afraid, Steve. My girl is far away. If I don't go to see her soon, I'll lose her." He showed me the letters she had written him. He had preserved the envelopes; I glimpsed U.S. postage stamps and a Cyrillic address with "Moldova, U.S.S.R." written in the Latin alphabet at the bottom. The most recent letter dated from over a year ago. The letters were in Russian; the latest one was written on the notepaper of a women's college in Winston-Salem, North Carolina.

"Your girlfriend's studying in the United States?"

"Her parents sent her there. They said she would be safer."

Safer, no doubt, because she would be away from would-be *muzhiks* like Andrei. (A *muzhik* is a Russian macho man; in contemporary Russia, Alexander Lebed was the supreme *muzhik*.) Andrei moped. A fresh wave of bitterness carried him onto the subject of his best friend. He showed me photographs of himself standing next to another young man of about the same height, his hair parted on the side, his features bonier and more high-cheekboned than those of Andrei's broad face. "He was my best friend. The best friend I've ever had. And he betrayed me."

"Betrayed you with your girlfriend?"

"No, Steve! My girlfriend loves me. He betrayed me with the Mafia. You work for the Mafia in Moscow, you can make money. You have money, no problems!"

"What happened?" I asked, not quite believing this story.

"*O mare problemă.*" Romanian for "a big problem," this was one of Andrei's pet phrases. He fell back on the words every time a television sale slipped through his fingers. Now his voice sank to a humiliated mumble. "He took the money and I never saw him again. The Mafia guys came to get the money and I didn't have it." His voice shrivelled, a formless grumble of sound. "They beat me. They beat me and threw me in a ditch. I had to come home to Chişinău to recover. *O mare, mare problemă*, Steve."

"That's bad, Andrei."

His energy rushed back in a drunken sneer. "At least I'm not like you. I'm going to make something of my life. By the time *I'm* thirty-four years old, I'm going to have my own apartment, I'm going to have a car. If I lived in your country, I'd have everything by now."

"You have to choose what you think's important in life, Andrei."

"No, Steve! You make money, you have a business, you can get what you want. You're just a failure. Thirty-four years old! Everybody else in your country has a house and a car and you don't."

"That's not true. It's even less true than it used to be."

I realized that meeting me had frightened him, opening his eyes to the fact that there was no earthly paradise. Not even people like me, who seemed to Andrei to have stepped out of a television screen, could be assured of effortless prosperity. I tried to explain that life could be much, much easier than in Moldova without guaranteeing everyone real estate and a car; infinite gradations lay between the two extremes with which his life and his television viewing respectively had familiarized him. But it was hopeless. He was too drunk and upset to absorb fine distinctions.

In the morning, as I prepared for work, I glimpsed Andrei sleeping facedown in the sewing room. Across the hall a large suitcase lay open on Dora and Senya's bed. Inside, a bright red Soviet passport sat atop neatly folded clothes and wrapped gifts. Dora was off on her annual vacation: two weeks at the home of her friend who had moved to Romania. She was taking Serge with her. The two of them would enjoy the hills of northern Romania and help Dora's friend with her chores. Travel to Romania was easy: Moldovans were admitted without a visa. Recognizing Moldovans as Romanians, the Romanian government couldn't justify controlling their movements. Thousands of people had moved across the border to enjoy the higher standard of living in the motherland. Bucharest, though, still couldn't challenge Moscow's cultural centrality in the mind of the average Moldovan. Romanians reciprocated Bessarabian skepticism: in spite of the sprinkling of eminent citizens who had arrived in the country as refugees from Moldova, the Bucharest newspapers delighted in portraying Moldovan "immigrants" as criminal scroungers.

None of this worried Dora. She couldn't have afforded the train ticket to Bucharest. She was taking her vacation "at home" in Moldavia; she simply happened to be travelling to a part of Moldavia that had remained within Romania's borders. I bid her farewell, knowing I would miss her and Serge. I had promised Valentina that I would continue to teach Borislav on his own. But after a few days Borislav stopped coming to his English lessons. Unable to locate Valentina, I assumed she, Borya, and Borislav had decamped to their *vila*. By this time I would have been grateful for an evening game of badminton, because living with Senya and Andrei had become an ordeal.

The Friday that Dora left, Senya came home from work carrying a plastic bottle he'd had filled with cheap red wine at a street-corner kiosk. Two men followed him in the door. The three of them squeezed into the kitchen, knocking back the wine at a furious pace while eating thick slices of heavy brown bread smeared with creamy white cheese. Most of the conversation was in Russian. I sat in the living room watching the evening news on TVR1. At one point I entered the kitchen to pour myself a glass of water from one of the bottles I had filled at the *izvor*. As I entered the room, the men fell silent. I nodded to them and left with my glass, closing the door behind me. Five minutes later Senya ducked into the living room. "We'll have to wait for the boys to leave before we have supper."

He looked timid and sly. I nodded. The men left an hour later. Senya, trying to quash his poor coordination by accelerating his movements, lunged around the kitchen preparing a cold supper. "I'm sorry it's late... Tomorrow we'll have hot food. Dora made me promise to give you hot food." He had changed personal pronouns, ceasing to address me with the formal *dumneavoastră*. I had become *dumneata*, a more courtly form of the intimate *tu*. I read a beseeching plea for complicity into this adoption of the formal-intimate. I wasn't sure how to respond.

Watching for my reaction as he sliced cold sausage, Senya said, "You have to understand that the boys don't like you because you're not from here. That's why I wasn't able to invite you into the kitchen...because of the boys. Even though they're my friends. My *very* good friends..."

I ignored his recriminations. I was learning fast—if a bit late in life—not to try to engage drunks in serious conversation.

As Senya finished making supper, Andrei arrived. When he realized

Senya was drunk, he stiffened. Senya began to lament Moldova's miserable, trampled history. Whether he was meandering along byways of his own imagining, or whether he had chosen the topic to provoke Andrei, I couldn't tell. I came to notice that when drunk Senya usually talked about Moldovan history.

"I told you I was born near Bălți, Steve. But my family came from Cetatea Alba, which is in Ukraine now. It wasn't even part of Soviet Moldova. Nobody knows what happened to the Romanians there. My uncles, my aunts, my cousins—nobody knows." Cetatea Alba (White Fortress), a Moldavian city since the thirteenth century, lay in the country's extreme southeast corner, where the Republic of Moldova now stretched in vain toward the Black Sea. For convoluted strategic reasons Stalin shaved off this southern fringe of Moldavia, awarding it to Ukraine rather than to the Moldavian Soviet Socialist Republic. Today Cetatea Alba is the Ukrainian city of Belgorod-Dniestrovskiy. A Ukrainian friend of mine would later tell me he had visited the city twice, in 1985 and 1986; even in those days, he reported, only people over the age of sixty-five continued to speak Romanian. Younger people had been raised with almost no knowledge of their parents' language.

"Moldova has just been a harbour for everyone else," Senya said. "Only Stephen the Great was able to hold it together. He fought forty-six wars and he won them all! He's the only Moldovan to have broken other countries' necks.. He *broke their necks!*" Senya illustrated this with his skinny arms and tiny hands, wringing necks high above his head.

Andrei snorted, gesturing toward the sliced sausages, tomatoes, and leftover rump of bread. We sat and ate, drinking sweet tea to compensate for the unappetizing food.

A few minutes later Senya resumed his litany. "In all of history only Napoleon is Stephen the Great's equal. I've just finished reading Napoleon's letters in Russian. If you read Russian, I would lend it to you..."

Andrei got up and left the kitchen. Once Senya and I had finished eating, Andrei stormed back into the room and bawled out Senya for his drinking. Senya shouted that he was an adult. What he did was his own business!

"Tati, you shouldn't be drinking!" Andrei's shriek verged on hysteria. I thought: *He's seen this before. His father did the same.*

Senya walked out of the apartment. Rain began to fall—a tentative spatter that settled the dust in the lots between the buildings. The drops fell faster, giving the dry earth a hard, steady soaking. That night cool air streamed in off the balcony. In the morning we all slept late. Senya surfaced only in the middle of the afternoon when a friend arrived for Saturday lunch. Andrei had disappeared. Senya prepared delicious stuffed peppers. He invited me into the kitchen. He and his friend drank beer and talked about cooking and politics. I listened, nursing a box of chilled banana juice on which I had squandered money at a shop selling luxury goods. The men's discussion hovered over the fate of conquered peoples. Senya's friend looked at me. "How do Canadian Indians live?"

I said that conditions varied greatly, but in general were poor. Many Indians were unemployed; Indians living in cities were particularly miserable. Citing a newspaper article I had read, I mentioned that the Native communities that had kept their languages and cultures experienced fewer social problems than those that had been assimilated. Faltering at the end of a long burst of Romanian, I said, *"Ştiu cine sînt*. They know who they are."

The men fell on my phrase. *"Ştiu cine sînt!"* Senya said triumphantly. He repeated the words three or four times. "Here in Moldova we don't know who we are. That's the reason for all our political problems. Now we have power and we don't know what to do with it because we don't know who we are."

"The Russians made us into their Indians," his friend said, taking up the theme. "Do you remember being told at school that Stalin was your father? We used to have a picture of Stalin in the house. I would get so confused about who my own father was. Why was this stranger living with my mother if that man on the wall was my father?"

"During the Great Famine," Senya said, "we were hungry *all the time* for two years. Or maybe longer."

"Longer. I thought the hunger would never stop."

"Finally we were given bread. Moldovans were told to be grateful to Russia for giving them bread—after they took away from us the means to look after ourselves, with their stupid collectivization."

For a while the men's drinking was hearty, full of a vital, anguished camaraderie that made me feel welcome. Once they finished the beers Senya's friend had brought, a strain of slurred desperation curtailed the rambling weekend quality of their conversation. Gripped by a bumbling urgency, they left the apartment in search of more booze. When they didn't return, I went out and rode a funicular I had discovered down over the treetops to a highway running along the edge of a *iaz*. I watched families cavorting in the water. That evening I was sitting alone in the apartment watching television when I heard a knock on the door. A slight, balding man in his late thirties whom I recognized as a business partner of Andrei's asked if he could come in to wait for a telephone call. Not having a telephone himself, the man often gave out Andrei's number. He sat in the living room, his ankles and wrists protruding from a dark blue track suit a size too small for him. I offered him a glass of water and asked him what line of business he was in.

"Clothes, textiles. I buy them in Tiraspol where they're cheap, then sell them in Romania where they're expensive." He shook his head. "Tiraspol's a horrible place. It's too Russian. They don't even accept the leu there, only their ridiculous Trans-Dniester roubles." He waved a two-hundred-rouble note in front of my face, Suvarov winking from the corner. "That's not worth anything. But Tiraspol has General Lebed and his tanks, so now Snegur says we all have to pretend we speak a language called Moldovan." The subject made him furious. He grew more and more outraged. "How can they say they're going to teach the children Moldovan history? It doesn't exist! Moldavian history exists, but not Moldovan. What does exist is the history of Romania, the literature of Romania. What sort of nonsense are they going to invent to teach our children?"

He collapsed into a kind of enervated post-tirade exhaustion with which Chişinău was making me bitterly familiar. He paced around the apartment, wondering aloud what had happened to his phone call. When he returned to the living room, TVR1 was showing a Hollywood film with Romanian subtitles. He glanced at the screen. "You can understand that, can't you?"

"Yes," I said. "It's in English."

"And you can read the subtitles?"

"Yes."

"Could you read the subtitles for me?"

I was confused but did as he asked. After a few moments, he jumped to his feet. "You see, you can read my language more quickly than I can." He waved at the television. "I can't read that fast."

"Did you go to Russian school?"

"No, but even in Romanian school we had to read and write with the Cyrillic alphabet. I can't read my own language. And I don't speak it well enough to have all the words I need without stopping to think. I'm almost forty years old. I'm too old to learn to read again...."

He fell silent and stared at the television. His phone call didn't come; at eleven o'clock he left. I went to bed. In the morning Senya and Andrei had returned. They didn't speak to each other. Over the next week the joviality drained out of Senya's drinking. He stumbled out of the bedroom each morning in a tank-topped white T-shirt and made me tea for breakfast. His eyes looked glazed, his body sashayed in an amazed, infinitely slow dance. Whenever his eyes registered my presence, they would focus for a moment with the expression of a disingenuous little boy uncertain what to make of me and playing it safe by being simple and compliant. Only the patchy rim of stubble clinging to Senya's sharp jaw spoiled his totlike air. One morning, too hung over to get out of bed, he squeaked directions for making tea at me from between his pillows. For the first few evenings of Dora's absence he managed to drag together leftover bread, cheese, salted tomato slices, and sausage into a makeshift supper.

At the end of the week I came in the door and ran into a gaunt, filthy, unshaven man with dusty clothes and a livid open cut crossing his cheek. The man was drifting around the living room, mumbling in an angry, half-comatose voice. I hadn't seen any homeless people in Chişinău, but this man looked as if he had lived on the street for weeks. "Who are you?" I asked.

Senya reeled out of the bedroom, wine bottle in hand. He looked stunned to see me. He fixed me with the long, perplexed stare of a man digesting an intricate, multifaceted insight. When the realization hit bottom, he took a step forward and shouted at the other man to get out of the apartment. The man looked startled. He stared in longing at Senya's wine, but Senya, brandishing the bottle like a baton, shooed him toward the door. Once the man had left, Senya retreated without speaking to me. A moment later I heard a cork pop. Senya closed the bedroom door.

At seven-thirty Andrei arrived and disappeared into the bedroom. A few moments later he entered the living room, looking very nervous. "Steve, I'm going to make a cold supper. Please excuse me. Tomorrow night we'll have a real meal. Today I've had big problems in my business and Papi is drunk."

That night and the next we ate salted tomato slices and brown bread thinly smeared with creamy cheese. Lack of food was becoming a serious problem. I knew the family honour would be destroyed if I offered to buy a bag of groceries, but unless someone went shopping soon we were all going to go hungry. Andrei gave me one leu fifty— about forty Canadian cents—and sent me across the street to the large, stark food store outside the development. Even here there was virtually nothing for sale other than bread and cheese. The cheese cost more money than Andrei had given me, so I bought a loaf of bread. The problem of obtaining food was more acute than I had realized. With the grocery stores so bare, meat and vegetables could be bought only at markets or through friends or relatives from the countryside. Dora had a network of suppliers, but neither Andrei nor I knew how to tap into it. What were we going to do if Senya didn't sober up?

That evening Andrei and I sat in the kitchen nibbling our dry bread—we had used up the last of the cheese—and dividing between us the final slices of tomato. Andrei was cursing Senya. "I remember when I was nine years old and living alone with Mama. That was the best year of my life. Such rich meals every night, Steve, you can't imagine..."

I could imagine all too well. My imagination was exploding into fantasies of delicious food. I gnawed at my final chunk of bread.

The doorbell rang. A timid woman with frayed hair and the quavering formality of a peasant edged into the apartment. She handed Andrei a bottle of white wine with a big Cricova label, a tall, thin bottle of dark Moldovan whisky, and a huge plastic bag stuffed with sausages and sides of salted beef. Speaking in Romanian, she said, "My whole family expresses its great thanks to Lawyer Lencuţa."

We had been saved!

Andrei, grinning and ebullient, spilled the bounty of the countryside onto the kitchen table. He explained that Senya sometimes did legal work for poor people. They didn't have the money to pay his fees, but months or even years later they would turn up at the door with generous payment in kind.

We dug into the fresh sausages. Andrei grew relaxed and expansive. "I have a big problem with my boss, Steve. There's no hope for me here. I'm getting my papers ready to go to Greece. I'll work there, save money, come back to Moldova, buy a Canadian passport, then leave for Canada."

"Is it so easy to buy a Canadian passport?"

"Of course, Steve. Everybody knows you can buy a Canadian passport. Papi has his contacts. For the right price you can get a Canadian passport made out in your name. No visas, no problems. You just land there and walk out of the airport. I know two people from Chișinău who bought Canadian passports on the black market and are living in Canada now. Of course, I'll come back to Moldova once I've saved enough money to buy a house on the edge of the forest a long way out of Chișinău. I need to get away from everybody!"

Before I could question him in more detail about the market in Canadian passports, the door opened and Valentina walked into the apartment. "Oh, Steve, I'm sorry we've been ignoring you. All day such hard work at the office, then out to the *vila* in the evenings and digging and digging... Thank you for teaching Borislav! I've brought you gifts from the *vila*."

"Thank you very much, Valentina!" I said, my submerged anxieties and resentment at Borislav's disappearance evaporating. "You're very kind." I opened the plastic carrier bag Valentina handed me. Inside I found nearly a dozen peaches, a handful of tomatoes, two cucumbers, and a plain white T-shirt.

Valentina left. Andrei and I cheered like children granted a favourite treat. Two gifts of food in less than an hour! And just when we were about to go hungry! We added the cucumbers and peaches to our emerging feast.

The gifts kept us fed until the end of the week when I got up in the morning to discover Senya standing alert before the hall mirror, pulling on one of the short-sleeved blue print shirts he wore to work. He picked up his leather purse and walked out the door at twenty minutes to eight to catch the trolley bus downtown. His first day at work in nearly two weeks ended early. By two o'clock, when I returned from my teaching, Senya was sitting outside on the bench. He was chatting with two scruffy younger men and didn't appear to be drinking. For the next two days he was snarly and introverted, impatient with the returning outlines of reality. He went to bed at eight-thirty and slept straight through till morning. I wondered again why he drank when Dora was away. Was he simply an impish little boy who felt compelled to be naughty in his motherly wife's absence? Or, as I was beginning to suspect, did he drink because he missed her?

# 10

# THE LOOK OF A STRANGER

"*Sînteți român?*"

People in Chişinău didn't know how to place me. In any crowd I stood out. My beard was a rarity. My hair, though short, was layered and parted on one side, in contrast to the crew-cut scalpings flaunted by younger Moldovan men. My pressed white shirts hung on a frame still gaunt from the marathon, meal-skipping eighty-hour weeks I had put in for the past year as president of my college's graduate-student association. My hiking boots and Reeboks came from another planet. I was a stranger and I didn't speak Russian. Could I be a Romanian? Was this what Romanians—those demonized neighbours from whom Moldovans had been shielded for five decades—looked like? I was asked the question incessantly. After having been the object of so many presumptions of Romanianness, I decided there was no alternative: I had to go to Romania.

I requested two and a half weeks' vacation. When I inquired at the office—embroiled, as always, in bureaucratic crisis as the officials typed and phoned to keep one teacher or another in the country—I was advised to buy my ticket to Bucharest at the Intourist office in the immense concrete tombstone of the Hotel Naţional. It was safer than lining up for hours at the train station amid hordes of dubious characters, and the reservations were more reliable. I walked out to Ştefan Cel Mare Boulevard and caught a crowded number 22 trolley bus. As I squeezed in the back door and gripped the overhead railing, I spotted a tall, dark-complexioned young man staring at me. A badly stitched-up circular scar veered out from his left eye. *"Sînteţi român?"* But, though he kept staring at me, the question didn't come. I twisted my neck, trying to judge where I should get off.

A minority of passengers stamped their tickets on the trolley buses. Most people stamped once in a while to ward off bad luck; passengers stamped when they were riding a significant distance. Sometimes the kiosks that sold tickets would run out, and no one had tickets. As I was travelling only four or five stops, I didn't bother to stamp. The bus rolled past the narrow, tree-lined section of Ştefan Cel Mare near the theatres and the fortresslike former KGB headquarters, perpetually crowded with shoppers and vendors of ice cream and fizzy, sweetened water. The boulevard opened up when it reached the city's one full-fledged department store, a spectacularly hideous concrete monument to Soviet architectural tastelessness. Many of the passengers got off, opening up a generous allowance of space among myself, the tall young man with the scar, and the four or five other people standing in the back of the bus. I assumed that one more stop remained before the Hotel Naţional.

I was wrong. The trolley bus rolled past the hotel and funnelled into the long, winding, downhill slide leading to the train station. My miscalculation exasperated me. I was going to have to slog all the way back up the hill in the midday heat.

When I stepped toward the back door, the young man with the scar moved to intercept me. His rangy body elongated by the stripes running up the legs of his dark track pants, he began screaming something about an inspection. I looked at him in amazement.

"Where is your pass? Where is your ticket?"

Not allowing me a chance to produce a ticket, he grabbed me

from behind. The hard pinch of his clasp stung my arms. He slammed me face-first into the back window. The other passengers at the rear of the bus, who had also neglected to stamp their tickets, stared out the window with supernatural concentration. I could see my neighbour's hands curling around the railing as he ignored the thrashing violence at his side. The man in the track suit, bigger and stronger than I was, flung me against the window a second time.

"Police!" he screamed. "Inspection! Your ticket!"

I had to escape. Even if he was an undercover cop—and wouldn't a policeman have had his scar stitched up more professionally?—he wouldn't necessarily treat me any less brutally than a criminal. This was a dangerous situation. I had to get out of it.

I tore loose from his hard-thumbed clutch, turned around, and shoved him in the chest with the flats of both hands. Taken by surprise, he was knocked into the pole behind him. I glanced at the back door. It was still closed. I ran toward the front of the bus. My assailant tried to grab me as I writhed past, but I hurled him off. He reacted with an incensed shriek. Peasant women clutching hemp sacks began to whimper. Although the bus had reached the stop in front of the station, the doors remained shut. I fought my way to the front of the bus, straight into the arms of three other young men in dark track suits. Two of them grabbed me and flung me onto the filthy floor. I scrambled to my feet and tried to dive past them. They seized me again, pushed me into a seat, and held me there. The third man, meeting up with the man with the scar, fell on a grungy-looking teenager, corralling him in his seat. Then they signalled to the driver, and the trolley bus's doors opened. The women taking their merchandise to the market in front of the station stumbled off in quivering silence. Before anyone in the crowd waiting at the stop could climb aboard, the driver closed the doors. The trolley bus pulled away again, silent and empty but for the feverish breathing of myself, the teenager, and the four men in dark track suits.

The stop in front of the station was the end of the line. From there the tracks drew a big hoop across four lanes of traffic, permitting the trolley buses to swing around and begin their journey back into the centre. The driver pulled into a lazy U-turn, then braked. We were marooned in the middle of the street, far from either sidewalk, the doors sealed shut.

The tall one with the scar strolled toward me. He unzipped a pocket in his track pants and flashed a sheriff's badge from a child's Wild West set. A plastic rhinestone twinkled at me. "Do you have a ticket?" he asked in Romanian.

"*Ba da*. Of course," I said, showing him my unstamped ticket. Seeing that he saw this, I reached for the meter above my head.

He grabbed my wrist. His grip, scorching my skin, reminded me of the painful force with which he had drilled his thumbs into my arms. He wrested the ticket from my paralyzed fingers and tore it up. "Do you have any other tickets?"

I nodded and gave them to him.

He ripped those tickets into pieces, as well. "Now you will pay a fine." He stared at me, his head cocked in a way that favoured the eye enlarged by the livid furrow of his cross-stitched scar. "Five lei."

I tensed with frustration. The money for my ticket to Bucharest was hidden in an inside pocket. In the pocket of my jeans I carried two one-lei notes and one twenty. I hated the thought of losing that twenty. It was only five U.S. dollars, but in Chişinău it represented two weeks' spending money. I had no choice. I pulled the twenty-lei note out of my pocket.

The man with the scar waved at me to put my money away. He was very professional. Neither the teenager nor I would witness the other's robbery. One of the other men closed in and pushed the flat of his hand against the side of my face, turning my head to the wall. They robbed the teenager and kicked him off the trolley bus. All I heard was a swearing grumble, followed by the clank of the opening and closing door. The driver, allowing the trolley bus to roll forward again, turned the vehicle through its crawling U-turn.

"You will pay the fine. Five lei."

I handed over the twenty-lei note. "Five lei," I said, indicating I expected to receive change.

They gripped my arms, hauled me out of the seat, and shoved me down the steps. The driver opened the door, and I staggered into the four-lane road where the traffic had been held up by the trolley bus "stalled" in mid-turn. I found my feet and stumbled to the sidewalk in front of the station. The teenager, his hands shaking as he struggled to light a cigarette, awaited me in front of a stall. "How much did you pay?" I asked him.

"Ten," he said.

"I paid twenty. I didn't have anything smaller."

He shrugged and drifted away into the market.

The teenager's aloofness prepared me for my students' failure to react the next morning when I told them about the robbery. The Romanian-speaking teachers asked which language the thieves had been speaking; once they learned the crime couldn't be blamed on the Russian occupiers, they lost interest. When I persisted, Natasha said, "Of course, you're the one they'll rob. You look different."

I didn't mention the incident to Senya or Andrei. They had their own problems: an undisclosed emergency called Senya to the north of the country for three days, and Andrei had lost his job.

Andrei's boss's patience had run out. The obstinately unsellable televisions in the sewing room disappeared. Andrei grew tortured and desperate. He sat in front of MTV for hours on end, then got up and scoured the apartment for chores, hammering at pipes that were in perfect working order to vent his frustration. He tried to expand his business with the friend who used his telephone, seeking a wider range of merchandise to buy cheap in Tiraspol and sell for a profit in Romania. All their schemes ended in chaos. One morning I woke to the sound of Andrei and Senya arguing in the kitchen. Hearing me get up, Andrei burst into the living room. "Steve! I've got a big prob-lem. You've got to lend me $100. I have to go to Romania in an hour.

Just give me $100 and I'll pay you back $115 in five days' time."

Senya, having followed Andrei out of the kitchen, watched us with an uncomfortable expression.

"I am very sorry, Andrei," I said in stiff, extremely polite diction. "I regret greatly that I cannot do this."

Senya looked relieved. Andrei crumpled and raged against his fate. All he needed was one good deal to give him the money to set up a nice little business. Once he had his own business he would never have to worry again. But he had no luck; good luck was reserved for others. One afternoon he came into the living room and spotted a copy of *Moară cu noroc* (*The Lucky Mill*), a tragic novel about a rural family's disintegration by the turn-of-the-century Transylvanian novelist Ioan Slavici, that I was reading with the help of a dictionary. "*The Lucky Mill*! I need luck, Steve. I never have any luck. The only way I'm ever going to get money is to sign on as a mercenary in Georgia or Yugoslavia. You watch. I'm going to go fight for the Serbs!"

He made the claim in the voice of someone who wanted to be dissuaded, someone crying out for help. Perhaps when he was older, I thought, he would realize he didn't possess the calculating hucksterism essential to the successful businessman. He was too direct, sincere, trusting. Andrei needed a society that would pay him a living wage in return for conscientious semiskilled labour. But he was no longer living in that kind of society. Such societies were vanishing.

"You don't understand what it's like, Steve. You come from a rich country, you speak English…" A thought occurred to him. "There are two Russian girls who want to meet you. They speak English. They keep asking to be introduced to the Canadian."

"Sure," I said.

I didn't give the matter any more thought, but the next day when I came in from work Andrei's voice called out from the sewing room. "Steve, there are two young ladies here who would like to meet you."

I walked into the room. The two young women sitting next to Andrei on the couch were tall, leggy, and immaculately dressed. They had avoided falling prey to the unerringly grotesque dress sense afflicting Russians of all income levels; their pressed skirts and white blouses were simple and tasteful. Their long, thick blond hair hung loose. Bright pink lipstick struck the only discordant note in their elegant appearances. Andrei explained to me that he had gone to school with these girls; they were his age.

As he was speaking to me, the more forthright of the two young women frowned. In flawless American English, she asked, "How come you learned Romanian and not Russian?"

"You don't understand when Andrei and I talk?" I asked.

"Of course not." She scowled. "I hate Romanian." Her taller, vaguer friend, who appeared to understand English but was less confident about speaking, nodded her agreement. The more talkative one told me she had lived for a year with a Christian family in Montana who worshipped the Good Lord. "You should have learned Russian. Romanian's not even a language. They don't have a culture. I went on a shopping trip to Bucharest last week. The only culture they have is Bran. I guess it's okay, but it's not very much."

I suggested that Romanian culture had more to offer than Bran, a Transylvanian castle marketed to tourists as Dracula's Castle. "They have an interesting literature."

"No literature can compare with Russian literature."

I asked about her shopping trip. She had travelled on a bus with twenty-five other Russian women, stopping off at Bran on the way. During her day in Bucharest, she had spent US$200. Next week she was going to Istanbul, where a full day's shopping awaited her at the end of the twenty-four-hour bus journey. This time she was hoping to take US$300 in spending money.

She paused. The two women leaned toward each other, locks of blond hair falling together, and whispered in Russian. The talkative one sat up. "Why aren't you married? When Andrei told us there was an English person staying and he was over thirty and not married, we couldn't believe it. Here a man who is twenty-five is someone with responsibilities, with children. A man who is thirty-four is old—he doesn't look like you."

"Obviously life is different in my society," I said. "Some of my friends are married, but none of them had children before they were thirty."

"Yes, in Montana I met twenty-five-year-old men who were like little boys." She paused. "And what will happen if you meet a girl you want to marry here in the Soviet Union?"

Taken aback by her reference to "the Soviet Union," I hesitated.

"There are many pretty girls here in Kishinev." She glanced at her friend. "There is a man who works for the American embassy who thinks we are very pretty. Many men think we are very pretty."

"I'm sure they do," I said. I asked them about their occupations.

"We are medical students," the spokeswoman said. "I grew up in Siberia. We moved to this part of the Soviet Union for the weather, but now my father is working in the capital. Sometimes he is in Moscow, sometimes he is in Berlin. I hope he is going to buy me a car so I can drive to university. I don't want to have to take the stupid bus with all those people. The university is so far away."

"It's only half as far as Botanică, where I go to teach."

"Oh, I would never go that far. You must think our cars are very stupid by comparison with your car?"

"I don't own a car."

"You must think it's very stupid to live in apartments and not in houses like you?"

"I prefer living in a house, but I live in an apartment at home."

"You live in an apartment?" They looked incredulous. I felt my worth slipping by the instant. Like Andrei, they could conceive of me only as a shocking failure: a Westerner too inept to have acceded to the natural attributes of Western life. Changing the subject, she asked, "What do you do here?"

"I teach my students in the morning and I teach two little boys in the afternoon."

"And the rest of the time? You know that there is one very nice club in Kishinev now?" Glancing at her friend, she said, "We go there sometimes. You can meet very pretty girls there—girls like us." Her smile glistened; her friend offered a demure but fetching grin.

"I don't really like clubs."

"So what do you do in your spare time? You watch MTV?"

"I read, I study Romanian, I take walks around the city." Seeing the appalled expressions seizing their smooth faces, I said, "I'm too old for clubs. I'm thirty-four."

"But you're not married!"

"That doesn't mean I enjoy the same things I enjoyed when I was eighteen. I'm interested in languages and cultures and politics. I take life seriously."

"But how can you? You don't have family responsibilities!"

Cultural impasse. We negotiated our way onto the subject of travel. How much of the Soviet Union had I managed to visit during my stay? "Almost nothing," I said, increasingly irritated by her insistence on resuscitating the U.S.S.R. "Ukraine's visa restrictions make it practically impossible for Westerners based in Moldova to visit Odessa or Kiev—"

"We're not very interested in your problems," the girl said with a pout. "We've got more problems of our own."

"And it's very expensive. You've got to pay $15 for a transit visa across Ukraine and $75 if you want to stay three days or longer."

She perked up at the mention of dollars. We discussed the safest places in Chişinău to change dollars into lei. "It's good to have dollars. You can buy a lot with them. How many dollars do you change for each day you are here?"

"I change about $20 every ten to twelve days."

"Really?" The two girls murmured to each other. A long, pensive silence ensued. "That's all?"

"Why would I need more? Life is very inexpensive here. The trolley bus costs only a few cents, most books cost less than twenty-five cents… I spend money on imported juices and drinks, but everything you need for daily life is very cheap."

"And you never want to spend money to go out with a beautiful girl?"

They stared at me. Andrei sat next to them, looking small, silent, and uncomprehending. He grinned into the mid-distance. I realized I had been very slow. The girls had been certain that, given a few minutes' exposure to their beauty, I would invite them out to a bar or club and spend my dollars entertaining them. Their faith in their own charms was both touching and off-putting, but not nearly as off-putting as their materialism and unreconstructed Russian imperialism. Deciding I must make my values clear, I said, "If I met a girl who fascinated me, I'd want to go out with her, of course. But so far that hasn't happened to me here in Moldova. I've spent most of my time trying to understand the problem of national identity in this country. I think it's intriguing that there are now two Romanian-speaking countries that are so different from each other."

"I don't think you are a real Westerner!" She stood and motioned to her friend to follow suit. They were both taller than I was; the quiet girl was very tall. I got up to shake hands with them, murmuring that it had been a pleasure to meet them. The formula seemed to mollify the spokeswoman. She looked down at Andrei, who remained seated on the couch. Her voice softening, she asked, "What do you think of Andrei?"

"I think it's very sad he can't find a steady job."

She nodded. "It is very sad. But it's also his own fault. We call him Parrot. He used to have a pet parrot. And every time you meet him, he's always saying, 'I've had such bad luck! I've had such bad luck!' He's very shy and he's always pitying himself. His business deals never succeed, but he still thinks he wants to make a career in business. In school he was always the best at drawing and painting. Did you know that? He's very talented, but he's ashamed of his talent. I think he should do more drawing and painting."

We parted on terms of reduced hostility. After the women left, I asked myself whether I would have excused their materialism if they had spoken Romanian.

# 11

# THE WESTERN BORDER

I almost didn't make it to Romania.

I boarded the overnight train from Chişinău to Bucharest on a rainy late afternoon, with the jabber of the public-address system, announcing the departure in Romanian and Russian, resounding off the rusting catwalks pitched high over the rails and rolling stock. A single murky sleeping car accommodated the twenty or so Bucharest passengers; more cars would be added at Iaşi, the first city across the Romanian border. A uniformed woman with a bad-tempered manner ordered us into our places. Our passports were confiscated. Mine caused an uproar. The woman scowled at my document, then called for a colleague. They discussed the matter in growls, resolving to separate my passport from the rest. "Canadian?" they said, as though offering me a final chance to repent. I nodded. They scowled again and withdrew.

The train ambled toward the border past herds of stringy-haired goats. As the red tile roofs of the last village in Moldova appeared, the landscape sprawled open in a pattern of long, bare gulches sliding away from shorn hilltops. A light drizzle fell. A farmer driving a cart down the paved road running alongside the railway shook his reins to steady his horse against the squeak and clank of the train, which stopped next to a line of freight cars. The shadow of the freight train deepened the gloom in the sleeping compartment I was sharing with a young Romanian-speaking Moldovan. His friends filled a compartment behind ours; as soon as the train stopped, he slipped away to join them.

It took two hours to change the wheels on the carriages, adapting the train from the broad Russian gauge to the narrower gauge used in the West. The power was turned off. I sat in the thickening gloom, staring through the rain-stitched windshield at the corrugated brown side of a freight car. I felt uneasy and eager to return to the West, to Europe—to enter a country I believed I knew, even though I had never set foot there.

A crash of doors brought my compartment mate scurrying back to his place. Voices bawled down the corridor in Russian. "Control," my friend whispered. The Moldovan border guards had come to check us out of the country.

In the corridor a voice shouted in Romanian: "*Who* is the Canadian?"

My compartment mate leaned toward me. "Watch out for the dollar detector." Elaborating in response to my confused silence, he said, "They have a machine. If you're carrying dollars—*beeeep*!"

Before I could reply two uniformed officials pushed into our compartment. The thick carpet in the corridor, absorbing the thump of their boots, had camouflaged their approach. They glanced at my compartment mate, interrogated him curtly, and ordered him to leave. Then they turned to me with grim relish, handing me a scrappy grey Soviet currency declaration form identical to the one I had filled in a few weeks earlier on the Polish-Ukrainian border. This time the questions were in Russian. I asked for a form in a language I could read. They found me a Romanian version and left me alone for a few minutes. I was still struggling to fill in the tiny blank spaces with information about how much money I was taking out of the "Soviet Union" when the two men returned.

The man in front, who wore three stars on his epaulettes, while his partner boasted only two, bent over me, placing his finger on a blank. "Dollars!" he said. He was fiftyish, his thinning grey hair scrupulously parted in the centre; his moustache rambled over his cheeks, black and vigorous. He passed my backpack to his partner. The other man, clean-shaven and beefily handsome, opened my pack and sank his arm in it up to the elbow, rooting around with a determined, hopeful expression on his face.

I hesitated over the currency declaration. I was carrying more than US$800 in cash—far more than was necessary to cover my expenses for the summer, though I hadn't realized that when I left London. The form demanded an accounting of every dollar in my possession; I realized I didn't know the precise amount I was carrying. Complicating my dilemma was the fact that my money was divided between two different belts. My large bills were folded into a zippered compartment inside the brass-buckled leather belt running through the loops of my jeans. Concealed beneath my jeans I wore a money belt containing tickets, documents, credit cards, and a pile of American $1 and $5 bills. I knew what a staggering sum US$800 would be to a Moldovan border guard—the equivalent of nearly three years' salary. I thought I should probably only declare about $200. But, stupidly, I hadn't separated my cash in a way that would permit such a declaration.

The two men watched me biting my lip over the form. The one with the moustache leaned over me and tapped his finger on the sheet. "Dollars!" he repeated.

Harried, I wrote: US$800.

The senior, moustached man read my form. His partner peered over his shoulder. As I had feared, the size of my declaration boggled their eyes. The senior man said, "Now we must count the money."

I remembered how the Ukrainian border guards had made this demand, and how we had avoided it by hurrying back onto the bus and driving away. But there was no driving away here. I unbuckled my leather belt, slid it off, and unzipped the interior pocket containing my large bills. Ignoring the cash, the senior man grabbed the belt. He had never seen such a thing. They passed the belt back and forth, marvelling at it.

The senior man counted my US$100 bills. There were seven of them. "You see. You made a mistake." He crossed out the US$800 on my form and wrote in 700. "That is your declaration?"

"Yes," I said, deciding to keep things simple. I didn't want them groping through the tickets and credit cards in my money belt. When he handed me the corrected form, I signed it. I felt a cool touch on my shoulder and realized I had been edging away from the guards along the bunk until my right arm grazed the condensation-covered window.

The senior guard said, "Now we will verify your declaration."

His partner opened a lumpy black bag like those associated in an older era with country doctors. He withdrew a U-shaped piece of black metal. Embedded in the back of the U was a transparent plastic switch. The junior man snapped the switch: the plastic lighted up, the metal prongs throbbed.

"Stand up," the senior guard ordered. "Hands against your sides."

I stood. My shoulder bumped against the rolled-up blind at the top of the window. For a moment I felt ridiculous. While the senior man observed me over his moustache, the junior guard began to run the twin heads of the U down the front of my body. The machine hummed.

When the junior guard reached my thighs, the machine whooped like a throttled goose. The white glow of the plastic switch choked with red. The guards stared at me, their expressions verging on fury.

"Okay," I said. "I've got a few more dollars here."

I pointed at the spot between my thighs where the pouch of my money belt nestled. I moved to unzip my jeans. They stopped me. "You've had your chance to make your declaration," the senior man said. "Anything I find now is something you've been hiding from me."

The junior guard pushed the twin prongs against my waist. The machine went berserk, shrieking and whining.

"Show me what you have hidden there," the senior guard ordered.

Unzipping my jeans as far as my haunches, I unfastened the money belt and handed it to the senior man. The junior man grabbed my jeans and pulled them down around my ankles. He ran the prongs of the dollar detector along my legs. Then he ordered me to sit on the bunk, my jeans still snaggled around my ankles, and take off my boots. When I removed the boots, he ran the dollar detector over them, then foraged in them with his hands.

The senior guard sat beside me on the bunk. He emptied the contents of my money belt onto the compartment's foldout table. Ignoring my tickets and credit cards, he counted my stash of small-denomination U.S. dollar bills. It came to $184. My total declaration should have read $884. "You're so rich you don't even know how much money you have." Disdain yielding to embittered professionalism, he asked to see the currency declaration form I had filled out when I entered Moldova.

"I didn't fill one out. I took the train from Lvov. We entered through Trans-Dniestria. There was no border control. Nobody asked me to fill in a currency declaration."

"It doesn't matter if there is no control," he said, his face a few centimetres from mine. "It was your legal obligation, once you arrived in Chişinău, to go and make a declaration."

They grew mournfully angry. Without an entry declaration, the senior man explained, they couldn't know how much money I had brought into the country. Perhaps I had spent thousands of dollars funding illegal activities? I laughed, but they interrupted me: I had tried to escape detection, the sign of a criminal.

This time I didn't laugh. The senior guard told me I had broken Moldovan law on two counts. First, I had failed to complete a currency declaration when entering the country. Second, I had made a false declaration, concealing currency from Moldovan customs. "We are obliged to start proceedings against you. Do you understand?"

"I've been stupid," I said. My leather belt lay on the floor; my money belt, tickets, credit cards, and dollars were strewn over the table. My bare legs bunched into goose flesh in the chilly, darkening compartment.

The senior guard lolled his head back against the headrest. "Yes, you've been stupid." He sighed, the momentary relaxation of his face loosening his avuncular moustache and softening the smooth runnel of flesh climbing to where his immaculately parted hair began. The instant of sympathy passed. "You've been stupid and that's why you're going to be charged!"

He broke eye contact with me, hunching forward. He was all business now. "The $184 you concealed from us will be impounded. Beyond that you have a choice. You can leave the rest of the money within Moldovan territory to be produced as evidence at your trial and continue to Bucharest with no money. Or you can keep the $700 you showed us and take the 1:00 a.m. train from here back to Chișinău to await legal proceedings. Either way you'll be put on trial."

"And I'll have to pay a fine?" I turned the three syllables of the last word—*amendă*—into a lilting ditty. In Latin America, letting slip the word *fine* was the recognized formula for broaching the possibility of a bribe. I waited for the senior guard's response. He gave no sign of having understood my overture.

"A fine or a jail sentence. That will be up to the judge."

I began to plead in my fastest, most whiningly supplicatory Romanian. *"N-am incercat să ascund nimic. Nu știam precis o cifră..."* Desperate to convince them I hadn't known how much money I was carrying, I pointed out that I had originally written $800 on my declaration.

"But when I counted $700 you didn't say anything."

"And I wasn't given the chance to complete a declaration when I arrived in Moldova."

He shook his head. Ignorance of the law was no excuse. "Stay here. When I come back, we'll go to the office to initiate proceedings for your trial."

He left in a disturbed rush. His partner, having lapsed into an almost teddy-bearish empathy, smiled weakly as he followed his superior out of the compartment.

Once they had left I pulled up my jeans, threaded my belt, and tugged on my boots in an attempt to haul together my dismantled integrity. Then I stared out the window at the freight train. The dusk deepened. No brilliant solutions came to mind. The idea of being prevented from travelling on suffocated me. My yearning for cultural familiarity grew keener. Bucharest, I had read, had been influenced by Paris; anywhere influenced by Paris wasn't entirely alien. I salivated at the thought of French pastry shops. Would I choose to travel on with no money, or would I return to Chişinău with most of my cash intact? It was no contest. My mind swarmed with schemes to procure cash once I reached Bucharest.

After half an hour, the senior guard returned alone. Sitting side by side on the bunk in almost total darkness, we argued through the basic points again. He was adamant: I could relinquish all my money and travel on to Bucharest broke, or I could return to Chişinău with $700 and a criminal case pending against me. Then I would face a jail sentence or a fine...

I pounced on the word. "Is it possible to pay the fine here?"

He hesitated. "No, not here. In the office."

"What do you mean in the office?" We were speaking in whispers. Down the corridor I heard an enraged shriek as a dispute broke out between a passenger and a border guard.

He looked at me, his eyes very dark beneath his grey-feathered eyebrows. We were sitting so close to each other that I could feel my deep, anxious breaths spilling over his uniform collar. "Where did you learn to speak Romanian?" he asked. "In Romania?"

"No, I've never been to Romania. I've been living with a Romanian-speaking family in Chişinău for five weeks."

"Five weeks and you speak our language like this? Who are you?"

He gave me a strange, fearful look. He seemed terrified of me, even as he continued to bully me. We were afraid of each other, I realized; neither of us could escape the menace of the other's power. He lifted his hands in a gesture of helplessness. "What are we going to do?" He seemed to be angling for a bribe, but I had grown too tired and upset to offer him one. He began asking me questions. Did I speak Russian? How much money did I earn? (Despairing of explaining the concept of returning to university as a mature graduate student, I had told him I worked as an English teacher in England.) When I demurred, he said, "Go on. Tell me how much you make."

"In dollars? About nine thousand," I said, choosing a U.S.-dollar figure roughly equivalent to the number of Canadian dollars I had earned during my last year in Montreal.

"Nine thousand dollars a month..." he mused.

"Not per month, per year."

"Per year?" He couldn't believe it. "That's all?"

"I haven't been teaching very long," I said.

"You know how much I make? I make thirty dollars a month. That money you tried to hide from me is more—"

"I didn't try to hide anything from you," I said. I could hear the strain in my voice. "I didn't know how much I was carrying. I was stupid, but I wasn't trying to do anything...bad."

"You didn't do anything bad. You've just broken the law on two counts." He leaned his shoulder hard into mine. I realized I had been wriggling away from him across the bunk. Now he held me wedged between his shoulder and the window. In a hoarse whisper he asked, "You're never going to tell anyone about this?"

"No. I've been stupid. Why should I tell people how stupid I was?"

He hesitated. His voice came out of the darkness, hobbled by self-doubt. "It's my duty to arrest you..." His shoulder pressed into mine. "You won't tell anyone about this?"

"No one. Never."

"Never?"

"Never."

"All right," he said. "How many Moldovan lei have you got?"

So that was it. He was afraid to steal my dollars in case he got caught with them. But Moldovan lei were anonymous. I answered his question. "Forty-one lei." Ten U.S. dollars. It was a huge bribe: a third of his monthly salary.

The train gave a jerk. He glanced at the luminous hands of his watch, then at the shadow of my backpack on the floor. In his left hand he clutched a long form: the paperwork needed to arrest me.

I reached into my pocket and thrust the wad of lei into his right palm. He sighed. "I thought you'd never do that. How long have we been sitting here?" He pulled his face up against mine, our noses nearly colliding. "You'll never tell anyone about this?"

His voice shivered. Now that the lei were in his hand I had power over him: I knew he hadn't done his job. "No one. Never."

He fled. A moment after the door of the sleeping compartment clanked shut behind him the lights came on and the train began to roll toward the Romanian border post. I faced the Romanian border guards as a wrung-out, shuddering wreck. Fortunately they were less harsh than their Moldovan counterparts; they weren't equipped with dollar detectors. Once the train had been cleared to enter Romania I stumbled back down the carriage to join my compartment mate's friends—a group of Moldovan men and women in their late twenties. The women were teachers of English from a provincial town. They had heard about the courses Theresa and I were teaching in Chişinău but hadn't been able to enroll in them.

I waved my hand at the men. "And your friends? What do they do?"

"Nothing. They buy and sell things."

It was the old, sad Moldovan story. They were travelling to Bucharest so that the men could buy consumer goods to sell in

Moldova. Relaxed in the inevitable gaudy track suits, the men asked me about my troubles with the border guards. They shook their heads as I told them how I had been threatened with arrest. They had been let off lightly, dispatching the guards with a pack of cigarettes each.

"But they expected me to have more," I said. "It's easier to be Moldovan than to be Canadian."

"It was easier to be Moldovan than to be Canadian *this evening*," one of the men responded. "In general this is not the case."

Their cordiality shrivelled. In the morning the young men emerged from their compartments wearing suits and ties. Businesslike and aloof, they barely acknowledged my greetings. I travelled in Romania for two and a half weeks. When I returned to Chişinău, nothing had changed.

# 12

# IRRECONCILABLE OPPOSITES

The long, hot summer sweltered beneath the cloud of the language legislation. Due to come into effect on September 1, the law split my class; the tension it aroused was never farther than a single ill-placed word from wrecking discussion. The Russian-speaking teachers such as Nelly welcomed the law as the restoration of their Soviet-era privileges. For Natasha and the other Romanian speakers the law represented the extinction of the dream of reunification with Romania.

In the middle of the summer, as the little dictators grew more fractious, a woman named Angelina joined the course. A round-faced Ukrainian of about forty with long, thick, dark hair, she had been a high-ranking Communist Party official prior to 1991. Self-confident authority concentrated the imperturbable gaze she dealt her peers from her wide-set dark eyes. A staunch Slavophile nationalist, Angelina lived in Tiraspol and commuted to Chişinău to attend the course. The other women were in awe of her. Five years ago they would have been trembling in her presence. The sound of Angelina's calm, controlling voice made Natasha seethe. One day, when my nervous (Romanian-speaking) supervisor was sitting in on the course, Natasha turned on Angelina. "You took away our freedom!

You forced us to speak a foreign language! You took away our alphabet, our history!"

Nelly responded first, her wrinkled elderly face looking sour with bitterness. "Your parents were peasants. It's thanks to communism that you graduated from university."

"I have four brothers and sisters," Natasha replied, drumming her desk like a podium. "I'm the only one who got a good education."

Angelina, unruffled, addressed me. "Stephen, do you know how many Moldovans were literate at the time Moldova joined the Soviet Union? Only one in ten. And look at the country now," she said in her even, politician's voice. "Everyone is literate and the children of peasants have been educated at university. What a magnificent achievement! How sad that those who have received the most can do nothing but complain!"

"One in ten! That's a lie!"

"It's the truth!" Angelina and Nelly said together. Nelly continued. "Romania never did anything for this country. Only Moscow and communism made life better here."

"Stephen," Natasha said, "I want you to know that many more people than one in ten were literate. We had a middle class here, we had a leadership, but they all died in Siberia. You send a million people to Siberia and, of course, there's no one left but the peasants."

"It's thanks to communism that your children are getting a good education!" Nelly shouted.

"Don't confuse the natural development of society with some sort of achievement of communism!" Natasha said. "Greece used to be poor and now it's rich, and they never had communism."

"People like you are intolerant," Nelly said. The chilling twist she gave the final word reminded me that her surname was Perelman. I remembered, too, that during World War II one of Romania's most brutal pogroms had been committed in Chişinău. Jewish culture's memory of the Chişinău pogrom remains strong; references to it appear even in recent novels, such as *Fima* by the Israeli writer Amos

Oz. "The Soviet Union was tolerant of all nationalities, but you wish to replace our humane communism with a nationalistic fascism."

Waving my hands for silence, I said, "Obviously this is a very complex question. I'd like to return to the vocabulary—"

I faltered a moment. Angelina, stepping into the breach, met my eyes, her head tilted to one side. "Stephen," she said in a deceptively quiet voice, "there is one thing I really do not understand. In your country there is a nationalist movement in Quebec. The whole world feels that if this movement succeeds and Canada breaks apart it will be a terrible thing. But when nationalist movements appear in our republics the whole world cheers and supports them. I find this very confusing. Why do you think this is?"

No one breathed. My supervisor regarded me with an anxious stare from the back of the room, displaying a glittering collection of gold teeth as she nibbled her lower lip.

I drew a deep breath, aware that my authority rode on my response. "This is a result of history. It's a question of the difference between the way Quebec joined Canada and the way many of the republics joined the Soviet Union. Take the case of Lithuania," I said, determined to avoid wading back into the morass of Moldovan history. "Lithuania was an independent country that was invaded by the Red Army in 1940. Quebec, by contrast, chose to join Canada through a democratic process in 1867." As I spoke, I could hear six million Québécois silently screaming that Quebec had been incorporated into Canada by military conquest in 1759 and that Confederation in 1867 had been a rubber stamp, an elite betrayal of the population, a meaningless watershed between two constitutionally different forms of colonial oppression. Fortunately no one in the class knew enough Canadian history to challenge my interpretation. "I think the world is always sad when a democratically constituted country threatens to break up," I added. "But when a country has been created by military conquest, then it's understandable for the world to support the conquered people's struggle for self-determination."

At the back of the room my supervisor was smiling, bulbous gold teeth aglint. The Romanian-speaking teachers looked quietly triumphant; the Russians glowered. Angelina made no reply.

The Russian-speaking teachers couldn't stand up to the Romanians' fury; if the bulk of the country's Romanian-speaking population had been as well educated and lethally articulate as Natasha and her friends, Moldova would have reunified with Romania in an instant—assuming the Romanians had wanted it. But for the moment the Slavs' links with Moscow continued to translate into invincible authority. Russian remained the language of cultural sophistication into which the ambitious assimilated. Nadya, one of my Russian-speaking teachers, told me she taught in a bilingual Ukrainian-Russian school. I asked her whether this meant the students studied in both languages. "No," she said. "It means the parents are Ukrainian but their children are Russian."

In late August, a week before the new language law went into effect, the national teachers' organization held a conference to debate whether the Moldovan language existed. The next day my boss's wife, by reputation an intimidatingly well-connected woman capable of securing the issuance or cancellation of visas with a nod and a phone call, entered my classroom. I had never met her before. *"Bună ziua!"* she said, introducing herself. "I am very pleased to meet you. The entire city is talking about your language class." She was a striking woman in her late thirties, her deeply tanned skin enhancing her russet hair, a dazzling white dress highlighting the prevailing duskiness. *"Doamne profesoare,"* she said, addressing the class. "Yesterday at the national meeting of teachers we took a position against the existence of any so-called Moldovan language. The language in which I'm speaking to you is the Romanian language—"

"We don't understand," Svetlana, a middle-aged Russian-speaking Jew of extremely mild disposition, said in Russian. Another voice piped up, confirming the protest. I looked around the room. The linguistic balance had never been so one-sided. Neither Nelly nor

Angelina was present. I counted twelve Romanian speakers and three Russian speakers; the results of yesterday's conference had persuaded the Russians it would be wise to stay home.

Faced with three Russians who didn't understand Romanian, the boss's wife switched. Her message that Romanian must remain the country's language was delivered in Russian. For forty minutes she harangued the teachers on the stupidity of the government's adoption of the "Moldovan" language and the speciousness of teaching "Moldovan" history without including the history of all of Moldavia. But the language in which she spoke undermined the message. The problem wasn't that some imaginary "Moldovan" language was about to overwhelm every conversation in Chișinau; the problem was the continued dominance of Russian, a minority language that had been enforced as a lingua franca. If three people in a group of fifteen didn't understand Romanian, the proceedings switched to Russian. Even fervent Romanian nationalists conformed to this custom.

In late August and early September, as the Russian civil service was spared and the Soviet status quo ante clattered back into place, no utterance was innocent of politics. I couldn't set the students an assignment that didn't provoke tempestuous debate. Hoping to concentrate on grammar and vocabulary, I asked them each to describe a journey they had taken. I deliberately selected a woman named Parascovya, one of the meekest and mousiest Romanian speakers, to lead off the discussion. But the mouse roared. "The journey that tears my heart is the one they prevented us from taking all those years by refusing to let us go to the rest of Romania, by cutting us off from our language and our culture and our literature, by telling us we spoke a different language—"

"But you speak a different language," Svetlana cooed. "You speak Moldovan." Nelly and Angelina were absent again, leaving Svetlana—who, like so many Moldovan Jews, was about to immigrate to the United States—to sustain the pro-Russian position. Her gentle character ill-suited to polemics, Svetlana greeted venom with schmaltz.

"When I look at you," she told Parascovya, "I like you because your face tells me you're a kind person. What does it matter if someone is Russian or Moldovan or Jewish?"

But it did matter. Parascovya was joined in her assault by Vera, a thoughtful, heavyset woman in her early forties whose dark hair fell around her cheeks in a wispy haze. Vera raged at the indignity of being forced to speak a foreign language merely to be served in shops and offices. "In my own country, where I speak the majority language, I must be able to speak my language in public. I am humiliated. When I speak Romanian, they look at me as if I'm a peasant."

"It is all one country," Parascovya said. "We must be reunited!"

Vera shook her head. "I don't agree. We've become a different people from Romanians. We speak the same language, but we do things in different ways. We're a mixed people. I'm one of five sisters, all of us married to Russians, Belorussians, or Ukrainians. The language of this country must be Romanian, but we must also recognize that it's now a different country from Romania."

I stared at her. In nearly two months in Moldova I had not heard any-one express such a nuanced vision of the country's cultural convulsions.

All the teachers returned for the last day of class. The advanced students insisted that Theresa and I team-teach their course for this final day so we could all enjoy a glorious farewell lunch. At ten-thirty in the morning, adopting their little dictator voices, the teachers decreed the class was over. Garbed in their best print dresses, they pushed together the tables in the middle of the classroom, spread a tablecloth over the top, and laid out a lavish lunch. The tablecloth filled with plates of sandwiches, pancakes of different sorts, at least four different varieties of cake, innumerable freshly sliced vegetables, caviar, wines, champagnes, and thermoses of syrupy-sweet tea. I shuddered at the thought of the money and exertion that must have been spent assembling such abundance.

We ate until twenty past one in the afternoon. Theresa and I were each presented with a handmade Moldavian doll and a musky-smelling woven rug. The teachers revelled in giving gifts. Theresa and I, responding in kind, announced we would raffle off our textbooks. Most of these were tattered and third-rate. By far the most coveted volume was a pristine book of English grammar exercises I had casually picked up in London a couple of days prior to my departure, never suspecting that in Moldova it would be accorded the respect owed to a sacred text. I had been told repeatedly that there wasn't another book like this in the entire country. We tossed all the teachers' names into a bag. Theresa shook the bag and I reached in and pulled out a slip of folded paper. Opening the slip, I read, "Natasha!"

Natasha jumped to her feet, her slanted eyes nearly bursting with tears. She hugged Theresa and me and grabbed the book.

Angelina turned away and looked at the floor. The mood in the room changed. I wished the book had been won by someone other than Natasha. The Russian teachers would never believe the raffle hadn't been rigged.

"She's very lucky to have a book like that," Nelly told me. "Even in Moscow you can't find such a modern English book. I think she has a duty to lend that book to all the other English teachers in Kishinev so we can photocopy it for our classes."

Theresa defused the emerging crisis by offering to sing a song in Irish. The teachers were intrigued to learn that English wasn't Theresa's first language, that behind her English-language culture lay another, deeper culture. Summoning a high, keening voice from the middle of her chest, she sang a mournful Gaelic lament. The teachers looked mystified.

"Now it's your turn, Stephen!" Rodica, a Romanian-speaking teacher, shouted. "Sing us a traditional Canadian song."

I responded with "Land of the Silver Birch." But the haunting exile's verses caused the teachers to shake their heads in disapproval.

"This song is wrong for you," Rodica said. "It's a very sad song and you're such a happy person, always laughing." She offered me a bottle of Moldovan champagne, urging me to make myself even happier. I refused, reminding her that I rarely drank.

"Come on, Stephen!" another teacher cried. "You can't shock us. We've all seen our husbands drunk."

I could imagine that all too well. My gold-toothed supervisor, suggesting an alternate task, asked me to make a farewell speech in Romanian on behalf of myself and Theresa.

*"Sîntem foarte fericiți să stăm aici în Chișinău,"* I began. I talked about our happiness until, confusing my pronouns, I addressed the teachers with the intimate form of the collective *you* when I should have inserted the formal. The Romanian-speaking women tensed; my gaffe was almost as improper as a drunken indiscretion.

"I think that's enough, Stephen," Natasha said.

Songs followed in Romanian, Ukrainian, and Russian. We closed our celebrations with a song in English. All the other teachers fell silent, conceding Nelly, the senior teacher present, the right of making the farewell speech.

"This course," Nelly said in her superb English, "shows us how people of different nationalities can work together. We have Theresa from Ireland, we have Stephen from Canada, we have teachers who are Russian, Ukrainian, Moldovan, and Jewish. But this doesn't matter. What matters is that we all have a good time together, that we all work together to make better English classes in Moldovan schools." She drew a deep breath. "A few years ago there were people who wanted to turn us all against each other. But now, with our new laws, we all live together in understanding. I hope this may continue."

The course had ended.

Later that week I went to dinner with Natasha, her impish rural parents, her prickly husband, Lucian, and her sophisticated, multi-lingual teenage children. Lucian, a burly, mostly bald man with angry curls growing over his ears, spoke no English. He showed me his sociological research in books printed in the Cyrillic alphabet. Natasha was furious at the way Nelly had exploited our lunch to make what she regarded as a speech in support of Russian imperial domination. I nodded in fervent agreement, then wondered why I agreed. What had prompted me to adopt the Romanian-speaking Moldovan cause as my own? The allegiance contradicted many of my other beliefs. Romanian speakers were more supportive of market-driven economic policies than Russians. The Romanians claimed to be fighting for ethnically defined nations, the Russians for multiculturalism, provided the various cultures spoke to one another in Russian. How could I feel drawn to a position that conflicted with many of my principles?

The one-word answer was: Quebec. The Moldovans' revindications sounded an eerie echo of those that had chimed through my daily life during my years in Montreal. The battle to promote a beleaguered culture, the humiliation of not being served in your own language in a place where you belonged to the linguistic majority: I had heard these laments before and had accepted that the answer lay in some form of legally guaranteed primacy for the suppressed majority language. I disliked the petty-mindedness with which Quebec's language laws were sometimes enforced, but I accepted the laws' necessity. I felt an emotional wrench at the collapse and withdrawal of Moldova's language laws. I feared I had witnessed the death of a culture, or at least the throttling of a potential rebirth.

But the affinity delved deeper. At the same time that I glimpsed reflections of Quebec's dilemmas in Chişinău, I also spotted flashes of Canada's problems. Living next door to a decaying superpower, Moldova was inundated with schlock culture delivered from abroad. Russian television bombarded Moldova with rock videos and B-movies. My time in Moldova had led me to a surprising conclusion: the most important fact about the globalized entertainment that was shouldering aside national cultures around the planet was that *its country of origin did not matter*. Moscow didn't need to douse Chişinău's airwaves with Russian movies in order to amplify Moldovans' cultural insecurity and subservience to Russia: Bombay talkies, Mexican westerns, and outdated Hollywood B-movies did the job just as well. The most important aspect of the garish dreams Andrei ingested in front of the tube lay in their insistence that life took place elsewhere, that the viewer's daily existence represented a simulacrum of the vital experiences enjoyed by those on the inside track.

The central point was not Russkie imperialism or Yankee imperialism—though these occurred and became pivotal in certain contexts—but the inducement of a feeling of powerlessness that rendered people susceptible to manipulation by more powerful individuals or groups, governments or corporations. Globalized schlock was above all else a lever for de-democratization. It persuaded people of their worthlessness, deterring them from demanding respect for their democratic rights or acting on the basis of moral precepts, local traditions, or the values instilled by a fulfilling experience of culture.

Histrionic nationalism—from Palestine to Israel to Iran to Serbia to Wales to the Basque Country to Quebec to Moldova—was a reaction against this alienating experience of culture, but it was also a barometer of how far "electrified earth" tactics had progressed. A city like Chișinău, ruled alternately through the centuries by the remote capitals of Bucharest and Moscow, the physical residue of its history repeatedly razed so that few pre–World War II buildings remained, was adrift on the planet's electronic cushion. Andrei spoke three languages, but unlike both his Romanian and Ukrainian forefathers, possessed no defined cultural tradition. Natasha's vehemence couldn't be separated from her guilty, estranging awareness that from her first name to her experience of literature, she belonged almost as much to the Russian culture she loathed as to the Romanian culture she loved. In both cases alienation had occurred long before the advent of the rock video. The crucial impact of globalized schlock culture had been to sap the collective energy necessary for individuals such as Andrei or Natasha to come to terms with their fraught identities in a context that lent culture—of whatever language—a sense of worth.

Nothing improved in Moldova after my departure. During the months that followed, the inscrutable president, Mircea Snegur, abruptly changed course. He supported a strike by nationalist Romanian-speaking students and courted the goodwill of the International Monetary Fund. But as in Lithuania, Hungary, and Poland, the attempt to combine ethnic nationalism and free-market economics led to electoral defeat. In Moldova, though, the result had dramatic consequences: it closed the door to reunification with Romania. Unlike any other former Soviet republic, Moldova, fleetingly, had enjoyed the chance to hop over the invisible line dividing East from West, poverty from prosperity. Had Moldova reunified with Romania in 1991, Chişinău might have been inside the borders of the European Union by the end of the first decade of the twenty-first century. No other city in the former Soviet Union, with the potential exception of the Baltic republics, could say the same. The cost of lost self-respect had been high.

# 13

# A DIVIDED DEPARTURE

**D**ora returned from her vacation to enforce order among her errant menfolk. By mid-September, when I came back from my travels in Romania, Senya, whose drinking bout had been succeeded by a series of mysterious absences in different regions of the country, had gone back to work. Andrei was coming home for evening meals. But a disappointment awaited him. Dora had found a job working as a saleswoman at a meat counter seven days a week from early morning until seven in the evening. Arriving home at eight o'clock, she announced that from now on she would be doing less of the cooking.

"There's no supper, Mama," Andrei said, stepping out of the kitchen.

"Ah," Dora said, "life is difficult without Mama."

Dora explained to me that she had hoped to turn a profit by hosting an English teacher, but the money paid by my sponsor organization—inexcusably late—hadn't amounted to much. She wasn't going to take any more English teachers. Her wage at the meat shop was an insult, but it might allow her to scrape together enough money to pay for a winter vacation for herself and Senya. They hadn't taken a winter vacation in years. Perhaps they would go down to the Black

Sea at Odessa… At the very least the job would provide her with her own income and occasional free cuts of meat.

Responding to Dora's stern command to assemble for dinner—"Steve isn't going to be with us much longer"—Senya, Andrei, and Serge gathered in the kitchen. They were joined a few minutes later by Andrei's track-suited business partner who had come over to use the telephone. This was my second farewell dinner. The first had been organized by my two youngest Russian-speaking students on August 25, on the eve of my journey to Bucharest. My departure from Moldova was split in two: I had said goodbye to my students at the end of August; now, in mid-September, I was saying goodbye to the Lencuţas.

August 25 had also been the day my boss's wife had entered my class to tell the teachers about the results of the conference on the Moldovan language. It was a day of hostility and contradiction. A traditional Soviet holiday celebrated by marches of war veterans commemorating Moldova's "liberation from fascism," the date's significance was ferociously contested by Romanian speakers, who saw the fascist Antonescu as having given them their freedom. On the way to work that morning I had noticed old Russian men wearing clanking medals hobbling along the sidewalks and filling the aisle of the bus. The war veterans were out in force. Chişinău's Soviet identity as a sunny spot to which old soldiers were pensioned off had never been more in evidence.

After my class, I took a bus downtown to the statue of Stephen the Great at the gates of Ştefan Cel Mare Park. A few minutes later traffic was cleared from the boulevard. The annual victory march from Soviet days was being reenacted with renewed vigour this year as the Slavic population cheered the withdrawal of the Romanian language law. Furious Romanian men buzzed around the base of the statue. They jeered as the Slavs stumbled past: old men proudly propping up hammer-and-sickle insignias, young people swishing Russian and Ukrainian flags over their heads. Watching them shambling past the graceful curves of the miniature Arc de Triomphe at the opening of the park across the street, I was overcome by a sense of violation, my Occidental fears brought seething to the surface by the sight of this Eurasian rabble trampling through the gardenlike setting of one of the central symbols of Western culture.

*"Ils ont oublié de rentrer chez eux, les Russes,"* a slender young man with Latinate features and a Roman nose told me. *"Ils sont venus nous rendre visite et ils ont oublié de retourner à la maison."*

I was sitting on a bench behind the Stephen the Great statue with tall, red-haired Tim, the young Englishman in whose company I had been invited to dinner. Tim and I were waiting for the demonstration to pass before trying to find the apartment where we had been told to meet our students, Elena and Sveta. Romanian-speaking men swarmed around us, addressing us in French, Spanish, German, and finally Romanian, grilling us on our views concerning the existence of the Moldovan language. They showed us maps in which Romania appeared in its interwar boundaries, with Chişinau safely ensconced within the country's borders, and other maps, bearing the emblem of the far-right Greater Romania Party, in which Romania encompassed Odessa and large expanses of Ukraine.

The presence of material provided by the unsavoury Greater Romania Party upset me. When one of the men showed me a photograph of General Antonescu, I could no longer keep silent. "I agree with you. Chişinău belongs to Romania. But why do you like General Antonescu? He killed many people. He killed four hundred thousand Jews." My estimate was at the high end of the generally accepted range for Antonescu's crimes, but even conservative estimates of the atrocities committed by the dictator's Iron Guard approached three hundred thousand Jewish dead.

"General Antonescu came to Chişinău," one of the men replied. "He came to Chişinău in 1942 and said we would always be part of Romania."

I looked out in the direction of the Arc de Triomphe in Cathedral

Park, on the far side of the boulevard. The Slavic demonstration had passed and the counterdemonstration was disintegrating. The broad boulevard lay empty but for tendrils of litter. The sun was sinking into the trees in the parks. I felt consumed by sadness at the fate of this lost province and all its embittered citizens.

"It's time to go," Tim said.

I nodded. We had to walk the length of Ştefan Cel Mare Boulevard before we found a functioning trolley bus. The empty streets felt eerie in the syrupy summer dusk; the two sides seemed to be hiding from the confrontation that would become inevitable if they stepped into the same place at the same time.

Tim and I didn't know where we were going. Elena and Sveta had been unable to tell us the name of the street where we were to meet them, or of any of the surrounding streets. They only knew the Russian names. In 1991 all the street signs had been given names drawn from Romanian history.

We rode a trolley bus into what seemed like the right neighbourhood, between downtown and Botanică, and wandered into a maze of low four-story housing blocks set at disorienting diagonals to one another, divided by dusty yards and enclosed by dense groves of trees. Children tore around the tree trunks in the deepening dusk. The apartment where we were going belonged to neither Elena nor Sveta, but to a friend of theirs named Sasha. Complex personal reasons rendered Elena's and Sveta's apartments unsuitable venues for inviting English teachers to dinner. Elena and Sveta had been the two Russian-speaking teachers I had gotten to know best. Elena was about my age, though she looked older. A handsome, shy, sometimes incongruously outspoken woman whose bright blond hair glistened on her shoulders, she had told me she had studied English at the University of Murmansk. Murmansk! The name conjured up English adventure stories about World War II that I'd read in childhood and adolescence: the convoys of British ships, stalked by German U-boats, sailing up over the top of Norway to bring provisions to the Russian allies through a remote Arctic Ocean port. "It was a wonderful place to study English," she said, her shy smile wavering. "The bars were always full of foreign sailors. They all wanted to talk to young girls and they all spoke English."

Unusually, Elena was a single woman without children. Most of the younger Russian-speaking women I had met were single mothers. Sveta was more typical. She was in her mid-twenties and lived alone with her four-year-old son. She had studied in Moscow but, like everyone else her age, lacked a full-time job; she taught at a language school for a few hours each week and took in private students. A small woman with compact gestures and short blond hair, she projected a prim, reproving air; single motherhood embarrassed her. She could be coy and elusive. In class she was almost flirtatious, but in private she retreated into unfathomable silences.

Tim and I located a block bearing the number we had been given, climbed the stairs to the second floor, and knocked on the door. An elderly woman who spoke only Russian answered. She invited us in, then admonished us for not taking off our shoes. We quickly obeyed her angry gestures. We found ourselves in a small, poor apartment desperately in need of renovation. One wall consisted of bare bricks while another was painted with a garish life-size mural of a tropical beach scene. The floorboards were rough and uneven beneath my socks. We weren't sure we were in the right place until Elena appeared.

Sveta and her friend Sasha arrived a few minutes later. I recognized Sasha, an attractive, intense-looking woman in her late twenties with an unflinching gaze and free-swinging dark hair. She had accompanied Elena to our class one day and asked to sit in for the morning. The woman who had answered the door was Sasha's mother, though I would have taken her for a grandmother. The apartment—two rooms and a narrow hall—was occupied by Sasha, her mother, and Sasha's two young children fathered, Elena informed us, by two different men. Elena's frankness made Sveta uncomfortable. She withdrew into a pose of maddening coyness, refusing to do any translating.

Sasha's mother and Sasha, whose English was weak, posed their many questions through Elena.

The question they were most eager to have answered was whether either Tim or I would be stopping in Belgium on the way back to England. The father of Sasha's younger child was working in Brussels. He had promised to send money to support his child, but months had passed and no money had arrived. Sasha was looking for a couple of men willing to knock on his door and remind him of his responsibilities.

Tim and I, saddened by the story, had to decline. Sveta shifted uncomfortably in her chair.

"Many men were in love with Sasha when she was young," Elena said. I wondered at the phrase: wasn't Sasha still relatively young? "Men even climbed over the balcony to be in her bed!"

Sveta made demurring noises in Russian.

"I think this is normal," Elena said. "Sasha is a very beautiful woman. But Sveta thinks we shouldn't talk about such things. She is conservative, like Margaret Thatcher."

We sat demolishing mountains of pork, potatoes, rice, beets, and onions. Sasha explained, partly via Elena, that for her mother the worst aspect of the past few years had been the erosion of her pension. "Before Gorbachev came to power," Elena said, "a widow on a pension could afford three return tickets a month from Kishinev to Moscow on the train and still have money to live on. Now Sasha's mother's pension is worthless. Sasha must support her. It makes her mother very sad that she will never see Moscow again. Even a person who is working must save for four months to pay for a single ticket to Moscow."

"What do you think of Gorbachev?" Tim asked in a soft voice.

"He is a murderer. And a fool. But, yes, he is a murderer. He has started all these wars where people are killing each other. My sister lives in our Georgian republic. The situation there is terrible. People are killing each other in the streets. And with the trains so expensive now we don't know when we will see each other again."

Tim looked up from his food. "What do you think of Yeltsin?"

"Yeltsin is a simple Russian soul. He is a drunkard, but he is a good man. And he is stupid. Gorbachev is intelligent, he is a competent leader and is respected all over the world, but he is a murderer. I am much happier to have Yeltsin as the leader of our country."

As Elena said "our country," Tim and I glanced at each other. Neither of us said anything. Sveta told us she didn't condemn Gorbachev quite as harshly as the others, but refused to elaborate.

We left at ten o'clock. "It's all still one country for them," Tim said as we stepped into the patchily lighted darkness beneath the trees. "Talking to them you'd never know anything had changed. They're still living in the Soviet Union."

I felt as bewildered as he did. This afternoon we had been in a stolen Romanian province, surrounded by Latinate men speaking to us in Latin languages. We had spent the evening in the once-and-future Soviet Union. Two mutually exclusive realities coexisted in the same streets. "We're in a country called Moldova," I said, "but no one here considers themselves a Moldovan."

❧

"Speak Moldovan," Dora told Andrei as he and his business partner launched into a desperate discussion of their latest failed scheme.

"Russian is better for business, Mama," Andrei complained.

"You know Steve can't understand when you speak Russian. It's his last night in Chişinău. Be polite. And, anyway, when we're at home we speak our own language."

After supper we ate chocolates I had bought downtown. We moved into the living room. Andrei brought me two carefully typed CVs and cover letters he and a friend—also trained as a mechanic— had had translated into stilted English. The letters were full of phrases like "Due to difficult economic situation in my country, I have not job at present." Andrei pleaded with me to take these letters to England and mail them to automobile manufacturers in Canada.

"Of course," I said, "but you should correct the mistakes first. In our society it makes a very bad impression if there are mistakes in a letter." I offered to circle the errors, but he snatched away the pen I was about to pick up.

"No, Steve. We can't type that letter again. We had to borrow the typewriter. It was very complicated—a big problem. Just send the letter, Steve. Small mistakes don't matter. Once they see we're real mechanics with a good training they'll give us a job and a visa. You'll see, Steve."

I shrugged and promised to mail the letters. Outside the window women were beating carpets clean on the large steel frames sprouting from the dust seven floors below. After I took some photos of the family, I gave Andrei an Oxford University sweatshirt I had bought before leaving England; Serge received a set of pencil crayons. I gave Dora and Senya an enamel plate I had bought in a handicraft market in Sibiu, Romania.

Serge seemed a little disappointed with his gift, but Andrei was ecstatic with his. He charged around the room, showing the sweater to Dora and Senya. "Steve," he said, "if I am to wear something of yours, you must wear something of mine." He took off his Russian watch.

"No, Andrei," I said, knowing how difficult it would be for him to replace the watch. "Really, I don't wear watches. I have a very nice portable clock—"

Over Andrei's shoulder Dora shook her head, signalling I couldn't refuse the gift.

"Thank you, Andrei," I said, taking the watch and clamping the clasp shut around my wrist. "I'll be very proud to wear your watch."

We beamed at each other.

"Steve," Dora said, "when you get back to England, will you have enough food for the winter?"

"Oh, yes—"

"But food can be difficult to find. They say the winter will be hard this year. You must think of the future." She walked into the kitchen and returned carrying two jars of home-preserved cherries. "You must take these."

I was touched. "Thank you, Dora."

Senya's face assumed an impish smile. He disappeared into the bedroom and returned carrying the best gift of all: a one-volume hardcover copy of Mihail Sadoveanu's trilogy of historical novels about Moldavia, *Fraţii Jderi* (*The Jderi Brothers*). Senya inscribed the book to me from the whole family. That evening, as I was preparing to go to bed, Senya returned to the living room. "Please be sure you mail those letters for Andrei," he whispered. "And when you go to Canada please look around and see if there is anything he could do there. You never know. There might be a job for a mechanic, there might be a way of getting him a visa... There's no hope here for a young person to have a job. *Andrei lucrează în zadar*."

*Andrei works in vain*. The words summed up so much I had experienced that summer. I told Senya I would do my best but that I couldn't make any promises. As I spoke the words, I felt a distance cleave open between us. Part of me had reassumed a Western diffidence, remote from the warm, pained intimacy of Chişinău family life. My head was already speeding back to England.

After Senya left, I opened my luggage and found space for Dora's cherries, Senya's book, and Andrei's watch. Natural abundance, Romanian literature, Russian technology: a more precise summation of Moldova's attributes would be hard to imagine. But it was Senya's final phrase that continued to peal through my mind long after my departure: *Andrei lucrează în zadar*.

# EPILOGUE: 2001

My summer in Moldova occurred at the end of an interregnum. In 1991 Soviet power had collapsed and reunification with Romania had failed. The country was adrift, too fractured to map out a course capable of earning the support of a majority of the population. By the late 1990s this nebulous period had ended and Moldova had been sucked back into Moscow's sphere of influence. The abandonment of Romanian as the country's official language in favour of the Stalinist chimera of "Moldovan" was a decisive step along the road toward a new era of Slavic neocolonial rule. The protagonists of this development were the so-called "Komsomol generation"—youthful members of the Soviet Communist Party who had been due to inherit the privileges of the Soviet elite when the U.S.S.R. collapsed. For a short time they had fallen into disarray, but with the onset of privatization they snatched most of the crumbs from the meagre table of the Moldovan state. Their resurgence coincided with the infiltration into the country of the Moscow and Kiev Mafias. The Komsomols and the Russian Mafia began to do business together and by 1996, when Mircea Snegur stepped down as president to be succeeded by Petru Lucinschi, they had become indistinguishable.

Lucinschi rode to power on the hope that his revision of the language law would serve as the basis for peaceful development toward a multi-ethnic civil society. He promised Russian speakers an end to talk of reunification with Romania, while promising Romanian speakers institutions where their language could flourish. Above all, he was expected to negotiate a withdrawal of the former Soviet Fourteenth Army from Trans-Dniestria. But the multi-ethnic harmony some internal and many external observers hoped to find in the Moldovan example would remain an illusion as long as the leaden hand of Russian power skewed relations between Romanians and Slavs. Once in office, Lucinschi, who had built his political career on a reputation for extreme caution and careful compromises, lapsed into passivity. His government said nothing and did nothing. Rumour claims that when Lucinschi asked his press secretary why there had been no press conferences during his first year in office, the secretary replied, "Because you haven't done anything."

Passivity gave way to venality. Under the umbrella of Lucinschi's government the fused ranks of ex-Komsomol businessmen and the Mafia carried corruption to heinous extremes. Prominent Mafiosi were issued passports normally reserved for cabinet ministers, authorizing them to sail through customs unmolested. From doing nothing Lucinschi moved on to doing business. His government developed into one of the world's great kleptocracies. By the time Lucinschi left office, foreign estimates of his theft from the Moldovan treasury reached as high as US$300 million—an almost inconceivable sum in a country as small and poor as Moldova.

The consolidation of links with Russia coincided with the decay of Moldova's ties with Romania. Many Moldovans' hopes were raised in 1996 when Emil Constantinescu, a centre-right academic born in Moldova, was elected president of Romania. Ironically it was Constantinescu, who had arrived in Romania as a refugee from Bessarabia, who would preside over the relinquishment of the country's claims to its lost eastern territories. In 1997 Constantinescu signed a treaty recognizing Ukrainian sovereignty over Northern Bukovina and the southeastern corner of Bessarabia that Stalin had excluded from the Moldavian Soviet Socialist Republic. In 2000 he negotiated a similar treaty with Moldova, recognizing the country's sovereignty and borders. While these measures disappointed many urban Romanian speakers in Chişinău, they exemplified a change of mood in both countries. Acquaintance had dimmed the reunificationist euphoria that had affected Romanians and Moldovans in the immediate post-Soviet period. Travelling in Romania in the mid-1990s, I found that if I mentioned I had learned Romanian in Moldova, the response would be: "And why do they call their language Moldovan? They speak Romanian! You learned from them and you and I understand each other, don't we? When are they going to rejoin us?"

By 2000, focused on bringing its national life up to standards acceptable to the European Union, Romania had grown weary of the waves of impoverished, semi-Slavicized Moldovans pouring into the country. Popular conviction insisted that all immigrants from Moldova ended up as menial labourers, criminals, or prostitutes. This prejudice squeezed out the facts, which demonstrated that some immigrants from the east became eminent writers, like Paul Goma, or even president of the republic, like Emil Constantinescu.

In the summer of 2001 I discovered that Romanians' responses to the mention of Moldova were disparaging. "I heard some of them being interviewed on television," one woman told me, "and if you ask me, they have Russian accents." Others claimed all Moldovans were crooks. Stories of Moldovans working as the advance guard of the Russian Mafia appeared in the newspapers. Romania continued to offer scholarships to Romanian high schools and universities to young Romanian-speaking Moldovans, but the economic ties between the two countries that had been forged in the early 1990s began to shrivel. By the same token, many middle-class Moldovans, having finally visited the homeland from which they had been separated for fifty years, returned disappointed. Romania had enjoyed so many advantages over Moldova, I was told. The Romanians had never been absorbed into the Soviet Union, they had escaped falling under the sway of the Russian Mafia—how could the country remain so underdeveloped? Why couldn't Romanians be practical people like the Hungarians, who had taken advantage of their freedom to create a more prosperous society?

By 1998 economic conditions in Moldova had become grim. The country's gross national product had fallen to less than forty percent of its 1991 level. The infant mortality rate had shot up to nearly twenty percent of live births; more than ninety percent of the population earned less than us$2 a day. Agriculture, the economy's traditional strength, had been brought to its knees by low international producer prices and endless drought. Negotiations for the withdrawal of the Russian Fourteenth Army produced phantom accords that were never implemented. A proposal to slice up the country into a federation died an agonizing death. The economic void of Trans-Dniestria—recognized by no foreign government or international economic organization and assisted only sporadically by Russia—dragged down the entire country, while Lucinschi's inert, corrupt regime persuaded many Moldovans that life would never get better. A British psychologist studying national levels of optimism reached the conclusion that Moldovans were the most depressed people on earth. By the turn of the millennium, some surveys were ranking Moldova as the poorest country in Europe—behind the re-Sovietized black hole of Belarus, behind dispirited Ukraine, behind even Albania. In the summer of 2001 I met an Albanian social worker who had learned good Romanian. She had done so out of necessity: she worked with prostitutes, and a significant proportion of Albania's prostitutes were now from Moldova.

The country that had grown so poor that its young people were fleeing to Albania couldn't get rid of its president. To represent a population that had once numbered 4.3 million people—a figure believed to have dropped substantially due to the mass exodus of recent years—Moldova boasted fifty-two political parties. Fragmentation prevented a clear successor to Lucinschi from emerging, so he stayed on, outlasting his mandate by months until the elections of February 25, 2001, tipped the country into a new crisis.

Observers both inside and outside the nation were startled when the Moldovan Communist Party polled 50.7 percent of the vote, winning 71 of the 101 seats in the Moldovan Parliament. Unlike the left-wing movements that had been elected elsewhere in Central and Eastern Europe in reaction against the hardships imposed by market reforms, the Moldovan party still used the name "Communist." The Moldovan equivalent to the post-Communist social democratic parties that had come to power in some neighbouring countries was Lucinschi's centre-left alliance, reduced in the 2001 elections to 13.4 percent of the vote.

The country's new president incarnated its contradictions. Vladimir Voronin, though a Communist, was a wealthy businessman. An ethnic Romanian from Trans-Dniestria assimilated into Russian culture, he had moved to Chişinău to build his political career. Voronin had campaigned on a platform whose "Communist" component had been as much cultural as economic: in Moldova "Communist" remained a code word for "Russian." Until two years prior to the collapse of the Soviet Union, no first secretary of the Communist Party of Moldova had come from Bessarabia. When the Moldavian Soviet Socialist Republic's leaders were not imported from Russia or Ukraine, they were Trans-Dniestrians, whom the Kremlin trusted far more than they trusted Bessarabians. The fact that the first two post-independence presidents, Mircea Snegur and Petru Lucinschi, came from Bessarabia had marked an important political shift. The accession of Voronin to the presidency signalled the return of the Soviet model in a new, more economically desperate environment. Voronin's fifty percent of the vote had pulled together thousands of starving pensioners, whose purchasing power he had promised to restore, with very high levels of support from the twenty-seven percent of the population that was Russian or Ukrainian.

Many observers believed, and Voronin appeared to know, that the economic planks of his platform could never be implemented. Moldova was an international pauper, its social policies dependent on the approval of the International Monetary Fund. Any move to raise pensions or increase state spending would result in the country's expulsion from the global financial system. On taking power Voronin announced he was leading Moldova into an economic association with Russia and Belarus. Even this measure was calculated as a signal to his electorate that the structures of the Soviet Union were on the way back. Whether the association with Russia and Belarus implied the abandonment of Moldova's intermittent efforts, initiated under Snegur, to build bridges with the European Union, remained unclear.

His economic and social policies stillborn by the Damocles sword of IMF approval hanging over his head, Voronin moved decisively on the cultural front. His statements and actions played to his Russian, Ukrainian, and Russophile followers, evoking key themes of the Soviet era. He denounced the Romanian flag as "a fascist banner," outlawed the teaching of Romanian history in the schools (though Romanian-language schools promised to resist), and mandated the teaching of the history of the Moldavian Soviet Socialist Republic— the version of history that denied the existence of the principality of Moldavia, which had consolidated its borders around 1350, unified with Romania in 1859, and had been definitively cut in two only in 1944. Moldovan children would be taught that the section of Moldavia between the Prut and Dniester Rivers had been founded and developed by Slavs. In July 2001 Voronin made his most dramatic gesture in the direction of cultural re-Sovietization. He passed a new language law, making the country officially bilingual in "Moldovan" and Russian.

When Voronin's law passed, I was in Romania, planning a return visit to Moldova. Beginning to feel that my arrival in Moldova invariably presaged cultural disaster, I listened in amazement as Voronin's press secretary explained the decision to grant official status to Russian by stating. "We need the Russian language for the same reason we need the American dollar. Both circulate freely throughout the entire world." The secretary's comments about Russian could have been lifted from the 1950s when Soviet citizens were taught that Russian was the global language, understood by workers in every corner of the planet. Had its import not been so serious, his declaration would have been laughable.

I was anticipating my return to Moldova with a blend of curiosity and trepidation. I had lost touch with everyone in Chişinău. For two years I had sent the Lencuţas Christmas cards but had received no reply. Once I tried phoning, only to be connected with a recording that blurted out: *"Numar inexistent."* I didn't know how to interpret the cancellation of the Lencuţas' phone number. If I returned to Chişinău, would I be able to find them?

For most of the 1990s, returning hadn't been a possibility. Moldova had retained its Soviet-style visa system whereby citizens of Canada and most other "nonsocialist" countries (now understood as countries other than Romania and the former Soviet republics) required a letter of invitation from a recognized organization, typed on letterhead notepaper and approved by the Moldovan Foreign Ministry, to initiate a request for a visa. In early 1999, when I left England and moved back to Canada, Moldova began to feel very far away. Not long after, though, I learned that visa application procedures were being streamlined for citizens of the United States, Canada, and the European Union. I would soon be able to walk into the Moldovan consulate in Bucharest with US$60 and two photographs and receive a visa later the same day. (One of Voronin's first acts on taking power in 2001 was to vow to curtail such madness, promising tougher laws for letting Westerners into the country.)

The last of my Chişinău acquaintances I had heard from had been Elena, who had invited Tim and me to dinner. For a couple of years she and Sveta had sent me Christmas cards. Later Elena wrote to me in London, where I was working, to announce she had left Moldova because there was no future there for Russians. It was as though she had finally absorbed that the Soviet Union no longer existed. Yet, having moved back to Russia, she didn't feel at home. She was living 550 kilometres north of Moscow. "It is very cold here," she wrote. "The winters are very long, windy, there are no grapefruit like in Moldova. I work at a school, but I don't like this school, because the salary is rather small and it was much more interesting to work at the English courses in Kishinev, because I met a lot of fine people, so I'm in great sorrow now, can't get used to Russia and the climate. All my best friends live in Kishinev." Elena's letter contained three photographs of her cousin, a gaunt, blond woman in her early thirties. The photographs looked wretched. The cousin's face, both excessively made up and too strongly lighted, could have been set on a mortician's slab. "Please be so kind as to show these photos to good men, unmarried," Elena wrote. Her family's only hope was to marry this blond cousin to a foreigner and pray she would send hard currency back to Russia. I wrote a difficult letter back, trying to convey that the unmarried men of my acquaintance didn't meet women through photographs.

Months later I received a short, pleading letter. Elena's life was horrible. Her salary barely allowed her to eat. She had no friends in Russia but felt unable to return to Moldova. She wanted to send her photograph to a marriage agency in America. Could I suggest a good agency? I replied reluctantly, feeling bound to emphasize that most of the men who consulted such agencies were aged, obese, alcoholic, or abusive. In the West, I wrote, with a prudishness that may have been insensitive to the harshness of her dilemma, mail-ordering a spouse from abroad wasn't considered respectable.

Our correspondence disintegrated into misunderstanding.

Sometimes I tried to forget about Moldova. It was easy: the country was rarely mentioned in the media. The figure who stirred up my memories, his photograph appearing frequently in the London newspapers, was General Lebed. His intervention in the 1992 civil war having made him a hero in Russia, Lebed was elected to the Russian parliament, the Duma, in 1995. In 1996 he ran for president of Russia and came third with fifteen percent of the vote. After dropping hints that he was grooming Lebed as his successor, Boris Yeltsin appointed the general head of the Security Council. Lebed surprised many Russians by negotiating a crafty peace deal with the Chechens, whom he was smart enough to see that Russia would never subdue. (He was a veteran not only of Moldova, but also of Afghanistan.) Yeltsin rewarded Lebed by firing him.

In 1998 the general returned to power as governor of the *oblast* of Krasnoyarsk in Siberia. His shadow continued to loom over Russian politics until Vladimir Putin usurped his function as the country's nationalist strongman. Putin charged into a vicious, costly, but relatively popular new war in Chechenia while Lebed squandered his energy in power struggles with Siberian aluminum barons. By 2000 only one percent of Russians supported Lebed's presidential aspirations; most had forgotten who he was. In the ultimate indignity a prominent institute for the study of Eastern Europe closed down its Alexander Lebed Web site.

As I waded through the breathless heat of Bucharest, I wondered what the border crossing would be like. I was plagued by memories of the two guards and their dollar detector. Once I had gotten into the country, I felt I could deal with anything. Getting in, I was certain, would be the harrowing part. My visits to the Moldovan consulate weren't encouraging. The woman at the visa desk refused my us$50 bill on the grounds that it had a wrinkle in one corner, obliging me to borrow money from a friend. The Finnish woman who preceded me to the counter was refused a visa. Finland, the Moldovan officials chorused in unison, wasn't part of the European Union! "But it is!" the Finnish woman said in English. "Look, it's written in my passport. European—"

Her protestations were in vain. The officials shook their heads: they would never fall for such a ruse. "You are from outside the European Union. You must have a letter of invitation!"

I was instructed to pick up my visa between three-thirty and four in the afternoon. On no account should I be late! I arrived on the stroke of three-thirty; at four-thirty the consular official in charge of issuing the visas rushed in the door. I had to hurry to the train station, where friends were waiting to see me off. At the swarming Gară de Nord attendants patrolled the Chişinău platform, reminding passengers they must have a visa to travel to Moldova. As I glimpsed the blue train with both Latin and Cyrillic writing on side, the peculiar suffocating exhilaration I associated with Chişinău swaddled me. I felt paralyzed by a human warmth inseparable from inhibitions, austerity, inertia, rage, and moments of violence. I slipped into the confined space of the sweltering sleeping car, dropped my backpack into the box beneath my bunk, and stood at the window, waving goodbye to my friends as the train pulled out of the station. The ugly, once-industrial outskirts of Bucharest sank into the low light. I returned to my bunk and waited for our passports to be collected.

It never happened. And here my confusions began. For weeks I had been reading in European newspapers about the ghastliness of Moldovan life. Yet as I approached the country's borders, then arrived in the capital, everything seemed far better than it had been in 1994. *"S-a democratizat,"* my compartment mate on the train, a thin, withdrawn woman in her forties, said when I commented on the changes. Whether or not the country had become more democratic, as she suggested, it had certainly become institutionalized as a country. My compartment mate wasn't carrying a superannuated red post-Soviet passport of the sort I had seen in 1994, but a shiny new pale blue passport with REPUBLICA MOLDOVA emblazoned on the cover in gold letters.

At the border the idiotic currency declaration remained mandatory, but the scrappy little forms no longer referred to the "Soviet Union."

Rather than being offered a Russian-language form and having to argue for one in Romanian, I found myself facing a guard who spoke to me in Romanian and handed me a form printed in English. The guards were firm but polite and professional; none of them tried to steal passengers' money or belongings. The declaration, based on the old Soviet model, obliged the visitor to sign the statement: "I must submit for inspection: printed matter, manuscripts, films, sound recordings, postage stamps, graphics, etc." I perjured myself by signing when I failed to submit my manuscript for inspection, but it didn't seem to matter.

In the bright light of the next morning the Chişinău train station was unrecognizable. The sign that used to say CHIŞINĂU was now bilingual in Romanian and Russian; the station had been spruced up and the platform was spotless. The crowds that used to camp out inside the station had vanished, and the ramshackle market between the station and the street where I had been robbed on the trolley bus had been converted into a manicured park. I felt I had been away much longer than seven years.

That impression grew stronger as I slipped into the Latinate street life of Ştefan Cel Mare Boulevard. Most of the trolley buses appeared to have rusted away into the scrapyard. Swifter, more expensive microbuses had picked up the slack of providing public transportation. The few surviving trolley buses wheezed up the street escorted by bustling fumes. The real change was in the proliferation of private cars. Audis, Volvos, Opels, Mercedes rode down the boulevard bumper-to-bumper. Who could afford such cars?

Everywhere I looked there were more material goods: more gaudy plastic logos; more stores and greater quantities and varieties of products in the stores; more cafés and more laminated menus and neat little napkin holders on the café tables, while the hair and dress styles of the patrons took off in all directions. This flourishing variety provided me with better camouflage than I ever could have achieved in 1994 when nearly all young men wore crew cuts and track suits and the sight of my Reeboks attracted block-length stares. I no longer had a beard, my hair was short, and my face had lost its boyish freshness and was subsiding into the anonymity of middle age. As long as I wore dark slacks and a short-sleeved shirt with a collar, no one looked at me twice. A second glance would certainly reveal I wasn't Moldovan, but in the thronging crowds of Chişinău's accelerated street life, who looked twice at a stranger?

I remembered an article I had read in *Generaţia* (now defunct, though numerous other Romanian-language publications had come to life to replace it) about an outdoor café that was staying open at night. In 1994 an attempt to create this sort of pseudo-bohemian ambience was a daring cultural event; by 2001 it was commonplace. In addition to the cafés and restaurants, downtown Chişinău was bursting with immaculate air-conditioned groceries full of imported German tinned goods and shoppers flaunting US$10 bills amid their wads of lei. The checkouts were state-of-the-art, featuring scanners and computer-printed receipts; no one now calculated change on wooden abacuses. My first attempt to speak Romanian to one of the checkout girls was rebuffed with a blast of Russian. The clientele for many of the posh new downtown groceries, cafés, restaurants, shoe shops, and hairdressers appeared to be disproportionately Slavic. Later, though, I succeeded in being served in Romanian in nearly every establishment I entered. After listening carefully, I detected that though most of the shoppers were Russian, some were also Romanian.

For the first two or three days I struggled to understand the pessimism about the economy and the future of the Romanian language that I had absorbed from foreign newspapers and some of the Romanian-speaking journalists and politicians to whom I was introduced upon my return to Chişinău. (I had more contacts now than I had had seven years earlier.) The city centre throbbed with economic activity, yet the Moldovan leu's exchange value had experienced a comparatively modest drop, falling over seven years from four to the U.S. dollar to twelve to the dollar. This threefold devaluation compared favourably with the twenty-fold devaluation experienced by the Romanian leu over the same period. (And even more favourably with the plummeting devaluations suffered by the currencies of other former Soviet republics.) Moldova had acquired much new wealth while being spared the ordeal of hyperinflation.

Not only did the city centre look richer, it appeared more Romanian. Moldova's institutionalization as a nation had occurred under the putatively nationalist government of Lucinschi, with the result that the large utilities (such as the telephone company) and many of the other major businesses (airlines, banks, cellular telephone providers) had attached the prefix "Mold-" to their names, which ran across the fronts of buildings in large Latin letters. In 1994 the only downtown businesses had been former Soviet state enterprises that saw no need to advertise. The few signs had been inscribed, mainly in Russian, in small dark gold lettering on identical black plaques. Now snappy plastic advertising blared out the existence of a multitude of services in a gaudy range of colours, and nearly all the signs were in Romanian. The McDonald's that had taken over the corner of Ştefan Cel Mare Boulevard giving onto Cathedral Park near the miniature Arc de Triomphe posted its menus in Romanian.

As the downtown building spree continued into the early months of Voronin's reign, new stores were being equipped with equally flamboyant signs in both Russian and Romanian, or in some cases in Russian only. The future was uncertain, and even in stores with Romanian signs it was easier to be served in Russian, yet a visitor could spend days soaking up the sun and the street life of the city core without suspecting the economic misery and linguistic strife that consumed many people's lives.

The Lencuţas' phone number was still listed as *inexistent*. I thought of all the reasons why the number might have been disconnected. Having noticed that one of the new microbus routes went to Buiucani, I considered hopping onboard and simply knocking on the door. But I wanted to try to phone first. One night, sitting in the modest downtown hotel where I was staying, I gave up on the Lencuţas, lifted the receiver, and dialled the number of my former student Natasha. She answered immediately. I drew a long breath and said, "My name is Stephen—"

*"Dumnezeu! Dumnezeu! Mamma Mia! Doamne Ferestre!"* Natasha exclaimed. We arranged to meet a half hour later at the Stephen the Great monument on the edge of the park of the same name. I arrived a few minutes before Natasha and stood in front of the statue, the sloping front of its stone plinth garnished, as was often the case, with bunches of fresh flowers. Pedestrians stopped and communed with lowered heads with the spirit of the king who incarnated eternal struggle against the oppressor from the east.

In the dusk I saw a microbus pull in against the curb. A familiar figure hurried out. Natasha had cut her black hair short, but her bustling energy was undiminished. She hugged me ferociously, then hustled me to an outdoor café on a tree-lined street behind the park. We ate under an awning. Over Natasha's shoulder a plastic Lucky Strike box revolved on a little platform. A miniskirted singer on a stage at the back was yowling an accented rendition of "I Never Promised You a Rose Garden." A young friend of Natasha's who worked for USAID came and sat with us for a half hour. At the end of the summer this young woman would be starting a master's degree at the University of Hamburg. She thought it unlikely she would return to Chişinău.

Natasha's life had changed as much as the shopfronts on Ştefan Cel Mare Boulevard. She thought less about politics and more about money. The year after our course she had taken the dramatic step of leaving her lifelong job at her college: "It was so easy. Every day I was home by one in the afternoon." Natasha went to work for an international bank, training fellow Moldovans to work in English, and was eventually promoted to office manager. Never having left Moldova in her life, she saved enough money for a family vacation at the Romanian Black Sea resort of Constanţa.

Later the bank sent her to London for a three-week training course from which she returned chastened, realizing her English wasn't like that of native speakers. After a personality clash with her boss, she left the bank and took a limited-term contract with USAID, where she worked under an Indo-American, whose hybrid culture—part Bombay, part California—had made her modify some of her ideas that identity consisted of one fixed entity or another.

When the USAID contract ended, Natasha found herself frustrated, unwilling to return to teaching English in a school for a pittance and restless to see more of the world. She cashed in her pension to pay for a two-month stay in London, where she shared a tiny apartment with five other middle-aged women from Eastern Europe. Natasha worked as a clerk for two months, then filled in applications, in her correct formal English, for other jobs. She was offered a position managing a small hotel and teetered on the brink of accepting the job but lost her nerve at the last minute.

Deciding she would miss her husband and children, she returned to Moldova on a cheap 4:00 a.m. flight from Gatwick. As soon as she got back to Chişinău, her restiveness returned. She found a short-term job teaching a hyperintensive English course for a medical school. Well-known for its high academic standards, the medical school had started to offer a degree taught entirely in English, aimed at students from the former U.S.S.R. and the Middle East who hoped to immigrate to the West as English-speaking doctors. Students who arrived in Chişinău without fluent English had to attain fluency within a few weeks.

"The course almost killed me," Natasha said. "I can't teach that many hours a day anymore. I'm not even sure anyone's going to hire me again—me with my Soviet English! Now there are many young people in Moldova who have studied in England or the United States on scholarships. I can't compete with people like that!"

English teachers were no longer imported from the West for the summer. My colleague, Tim, had come back and worked in Chişinău for one more summer; after that the program was closed down. My former boss and his wife had founded a private school where the new elite could spend its dubiously gained wealth educating its children into respectability. My teaching partner, Theresa, had tried to return to Chişinău as a tourist but had been denied a visa. She had phoned Natasha from Iaşi, Romania, crying into the telephone that this was her last trip outside Ireland, she was too old to keep travelling, and now she would never be able to return to her beloved "Moldava."

Westerners had become less of a novelty in Chişinău: there were development workers, aid projects, and born-again missionaries galore. But Natasha, like others with whom I renewed contact, remembered that I had been the first Westerner she had gotten to know after the Soviet Union disintegrated. She still recalled the text-book she had won in the lottery at the end of the course—"that you gave me," she said, making me feel uncomfortable. Yet she barely acknowledged the more expensive advanced textbook I had brought her this time as a gift. Seven years of commercialization had smoothed down many of the differences between my culture and Natasha's. At the same time exposure to the West had heightened Natasha's awareness of the differences that remained. Her loss of confidence in her excellent if traditional English was the most obvious sign of this: in 1994 we had spoken exclusively in English; now we spoke only in Romanian.

We talked about her family and about money. Her only reference to the Russians was to chide me that by not learning Russian I was missing the opportunity to read the world's greatest literature in the original. A few days later, when I went to lunch at her apartment, she muttered, "I have nothing against links with the Russians as long as we can be ourselves." For most of the evening at the café we discussed her daughter, whom I remembered as a bewitching, sloe-eyed twelve-year-old fluent in four languages. Now nineteen and fluent in six languages, Natasha's daughter had gone to Germany to work as an au pair and had returned engaged to marry a thirty-nine-year-old U.S. Army officer. "*Un baiat bun*, a good boy," Natasha murmured, trying to console herself. "He seems like a boy. He's not like a man his age would be here. But, oh, I worry so much. His next posting may be to Japan for three years. Does this mean my daughter will never go to university? She's so intelligent. She must go to university! Of course, you have to let them make their own decisions. In your countries do people often get married when there's that kind of age difference?"

"No," I said. "Not often." I learned that Natasha's daughter had been working in Hamburg while her fiancé had been stationed at a NATO base in southern Germany. They had known each other for only a few days when they decided to get married.

My face must have betrayed my misgivings, because Natasha said, "That's how my husband reacted, too. When she came back to visit—*oh la la!* You know how the daughter is always special to the father and the first time he knows she has been with a man he is jealous? It was horrible!"

Natasha's husband's personality wouldn't have made this encounter any easier. I was reminded of Lucian's demanding gruffness later in the week. He had grown stouter in the past seven years and was now completely bald on top, the ruffs of hair around his ears thinned to a powdery whiteness. Over lunch at their comfortable apartment he asked me what I thought of the changes in Chişinău. I replied I was impressed by the new shops downtown but wondered what proportion of the population could afford to patronize them.

"Seven percent," Lucian said. "I've researched it." What did I think of the fundamentalist Christian missionaries? he asked. I mumbled a perfunctory response. He pulled out a wall-size map of the country shaded in to present the data he had compiled on rates of conversion to Baptism, Mormonism, and the Jehovah's Witnesses in every town in Moldova. The map was in Russian. His research was in Russian, even though much of it was devoted to examining the lack of opportunities for speakers of Romanian. Aware there were many Ukrainians in Canada, he asked whether there was a university in my country where he could teach in Ukrainian. Was scholarly research taken seriously in a country like Canada? If he wrote his articles in Romanian instead of Russian, could I translate them for him and publish them in Canada? The interrogation, conducted beneath two enormous photographs of his vanished daughter looking beautiful and elated against famous Western European backdrops, grew tenser and more aggressive. Why wasn't I willing to publish his articles in Canada for him?

"You should try in Romania," Natasha said. "It's the same linguistic space."

"Romania! Do you think that country will ever go anywhere? They don't know how to work the way we Bessarabians do."

"That means we could get to the top quickly there," Natasha said. "We know the language and we know how to work."

As the afternoon progressed, I saw that Lucian's and Natasha's differing anxieties were chafing each other. Like many East European men—even men who had defined themselves in opposition to the power structures of the old order—Lucian feared the libertarianism preached by global mass culture. Globalization meant he could no longer keep his womenfolk under control. His daughter had run off to Germany and was marrying an American, while his wife, having disappeared to London for two months, had declared her eagerness to take off again. His status as a university professor no longer commanded the respect that had once been his due. The kind of knowledge he possessed had become less admired than street know-how.

Lucian earned nine hundred lei (US$75) a month, a decent salary by Moldovan standards, but a mere trickle by comparison with the stacks of dollars accumulated by half-educated entrepreneurs who lived with one foot on either side of the law. He spoke three languages—Romanian, Russian, and Ukrainian—but they were all eastern languages. He knew not a word of the other languages globalization was making important: English, above all, but to a lesser extent German. Within the trade-oriented context of post–Cold War

Eurasia, even Turkish would have provided him with more mobility. He was too proud and prickly, too stolidly ensconced in his throne as a conferer of wisdom, to subject himself to the indignity of wrestling with a new language or becoming an immigrant.

Natasha, meanwhile, saw departure from Moldova as her only hope to avoid an impoverished old age. "Stephen, my parents are living on a pension of two hundred and fifty lei a month. It's a better pension than many old people have, but I don't want to live like that. I've just turned fifty. I have ten years to save for my old age. I can only do it if I earn in foreign currency."

I thought about a pension of two hundred and fifty lei (US$21); at the café my share of the bill, which Natasha had insisted on paying, had come to more than fifty lei. Natasha made a quick joke in English. It was just a sentence, but Lucian bristled. "What did you say? What did you say in English?" Natasha explained the joke. As the conversation continued, she hesitated twice to ask Lucian for the Romanian translations of Russian words. I couldn't work out whether she had really forgotten the words, or whether this was her way of mollifying her husband by deferring to his authority.

Lucian interrogated me on the subject of universities in Western Europe. Were they as serious as Moldovan universities? Would they be respectable places to work? What did I think of the Central European University? I said I had only seen the Budapest branch, not the main campus in Prague, but that I had heard it was an excellent university. Lucian looked at me with an expression that blended longing and skepticism. He shrugged. "But you probably have to teach in English... There's no hope."

"Whatever we do in another country," Natasha said, "we will earn more money than we would in Moldova."

While their daughter gazed down from the photographs with a riddle of a smile promising the solution to the mystery of the contemporary world, Natasha and Lucian's son looked up in silence from his post at the living-room table. A quiet young man who had inherited Natasha's Latinate looks but a shyer version of Lucian's uncomfortable personality, he wore a T-shirt bearing the slogan DROGURILOR NU! (NO TO DRUGS!). He was finishing law school. "He will apply for a job in the civil service," Lucian said, while the boy sat silent. "There he will earn a decent salary."

I envisaged him emulating his father by clinging to unravelling, underachieving respectability while the women of the family moved on. "The next time you come back," Natasha said, "we may not be here."

Lucian sighed.

My sun-struck idyll faded. One evening on my way back down Ştefan Cel Mare Boulevard to my hotel I noticed a semicircle of soldiers standing under the red awning of a bar near the former KGB head-quarters. The awning was dominated by a large Coca-Cola logo, providing the impression that the young soldiers were slouching in a circular queue in the hope of getting a sip of the defining brew of the West. Only as I tried to slip around them did I see the body. A man lay on his back on the sidewalk. The soldiers had tossed a tartan blanket over him, concealing him from his forehead to his shins. The unnatural parallel bars of his ankles—sockless and leading to petite black boots—stuck out from beneath the red and black patterns of the wool. I wondered fleetingly why soldiers and not the police were attending this death. The muscular young men sitting at the café's out-door tables ignored the body and spoke on their mobile telephones.

There were cafés everywhere. In the corner of the parking lot in front of my hotel a modest café had been assembled by pushing together a couple of freezer units, a stall, white circular tables equipped with parasols, and a bevy of white plastic chairs. The café was always full. The evening after the day I had seen the body in the street I was returning from a search for an Internet café. It was eight o'clock, the heat was crushing, and I felt parched. Crossing the parking lot, I decided to buy a drink, changed course, and headed for the café. As I drew near, two large crew-cut men in white T-shirts stood and began punching each other. The slap of knuckles on broad biceps brought me to a halt. The fight was clumsy and brutal. One by one the other men in the café rose and looked around with tense fear. Some of them began punching, as well. The first blows lacked vigour, but once a man had been belted in the shoulder or slapped across the face his ire increased. One of the two men who had started the fight picked up his chair and smashed another man over the head with incredible, hateful force. When somebody lunged at the man with the chair, I edged toward the hotel.

A loud shout broke from the hotel's front door. A small car pulled up and men wearing black T-shirts and black motorcycle-style helmets swarmed out and surrounded the fighters. Two men broke away from the brawl and ran flat-out toward the hotel. One held his hand across his mouth to catch dripping blood. The other ran barefoot, clutching his shoes. A moment later a second small white car arrived and more men in black T-shirts and black helmets got out. Two of these men were carrying AK-47s. I continued to sidestep in the direction of the hotel. The men in black T-shirts weren't police, yet they didn't show the slightest hesitation in levelling their carbines on the brawlers, corralling the men with police-style nightsticks, and interrogating them. I retreated to my third-floor room overlooking the café. From my window I saw the interrogation continue for twenty minutes as evening deepened into night. Then, responding to an unseen signal, everyone—brawlers, men in black, attendants—left. The café closed for the evening. The next day it was sparsely frequented, but by the day after everything was back to normal.

I assumed I had witnessed the intervention of a private security team in a gangland brawl, but I couldn't be sure. Authority was untraceable in contemporary Moldova. No one knew who was in charge or why some procedures worked while others did not. One night directory assistance stunned me by coughing up a phone number for the Lencuţas. I dialled this number at different times of day over a two-day period. No answer.

The next afternoon I went out for a long walk through the market and the narrow streets of the former Jewish district down the hill behind Ştefan Cel Mare Boulevard. By the time I returned to my hotel room, my shirt was no longer a shirt but a sodden rag. I pulled it off and fell asleep, only to awake sneezing into the dusk. The sweat on my torso had dried and turned cold. The parking lot beneath my window was dark but for the glow of the café. With an automaton-like movement I reached for the telephone and dialled the Lencuţas' number. The phone was answered by a woman's voice on the second ring. "*Alo,*" I said. A cavernous silence. "*Alo?*" I repeated. "Dora?"

This time the silence was even longer. "Steve? Steve...?"

"Dora?"

"Yes, yes, it's Dora. Where are you, Steve? Are you in England? Are you in Romania?"

Still groggy, I blinked out the window at the darkened parking lot. Could this be happening? Had I really gotten back in touch with the Lencuţas? "I'm in a hotel in the centre of town."

"What are you doing in a hotel? How can you come to Chişinău and stay in a hotel? Come sleep at my place. Come right now! I want to talk to you."

"I want to talk to you, too. But it's late, Dora. I'll come tomorrow."

"It's not late! I want to talk to you. Steve, if you don't come now, I'll come to the hotel and take you away!"

We argued for ten minutes. I agreed to come to Buiucani for a short visit, then return the next day with my luggage. When I put down the receiver, I got up, washed my face in the basin, and hunted for a shirt that hadn't been crumpled by sweat. I left the hotel, crossed the darkened street, and hailed a 3A microbus to Buiucani. As the van moved by fits and starts down the long boulevard, I observed that the transition from trolley bus to microbus had brought with it a change in linguistic culture. On the trolley buses squeezed-together passengers would find out who was getting off at the next stop by rhyming off the Romanian sequence "*Coborîţi?*"..."*Da, cobor*" ("Are you getting off?"..."Yes, I'm getting off"). In the microbuses even passengers who spoke to each other in Romanian would use Russian to ask the driver to stop. Consultation on the trolley buses took place among passengers presumed to be equals, hence the majority language could be used. On the microbuses passengers spoke to the driver: as a public official, the driver was addressed in Russian.

As the van crawled around the traffic circle at the bottom of Ştefan Cel Mare Boulevard and began the long climb up the hill toward Buiucani, I saw that the commercial wave had rolled far from the city's core. Even in these modest residential neighbourhoods, there were small shops, snappy plastic signs, familiar transnational logos. The van wound up the hill the back way, approaching Buiucani through the trees. The hilltop wall of apartment blocks defining the district's perimeter didn't soar so high from this angle. It was dark when I got down from the microbus. The old state-run grocery store outside the development, which I remembered as stocking only bread and vodka, had been refurbished with glaring red trim and was renamed—in English—"Victoria Market." A scattering of café tables spread away from the front door: even the shopping centre had become a place to sit outdoors in the evening.

Across the street, in the shadow of the wall of apartment blocks, the outlook had changed much less. The darkness would have been impenetrable but for the row of kiosks, most of them illumined by the flat light of generators. In the murk at the base of the buildings crowds of young people hung out on concrete blocks or sprawled on the dry grass. They drank, flirted, and played with young children. Under the glow slicking the counter of a kiosk I noticed a middle-aged man hand over rumpled lei to the attendant, who filled a soft-drink bottle with wine. The man took the bottle and hurried into the darkness as my microbus pulled away.

I walked through the night, confident I would remain anonymous as long as I seemed to know where I was going. A child crossed my path, and a teenage girl shouted at the toddler in Russian. As my eyes adjusted to the deep shadow, I made out a heavyset woman with a mop of dyed blond hair and a collapsed face standing at the corner behind the last kiosk. I glanced away, then looked back and saw her continue to peer into the gloom. Children, teenagers, and drunks moved around the woman, who stared past me. I walked toward her, squinting to recover features I remembered. It was Dora. Finally she saw me coming, looked nervous at my approach, then relaxed.

After she shook my hand, she pulled it close to her, and I was struck by how much less physical she was than Natasha, who had embraced me in front of the Stephen the Great statue. I became conscious of traits I had forgotten: Dora's wariness, her formal, poor woman's reserve, her concern for maintaining appearances. We had barely met when she explained that her face was puffy because it was allergy season; next week, when she went to the hospital for her shots, she would look better.

We walked around the back of the row of high-rise blocks. The ground felt rougher and more pitted than I remembered. "You've changed," Dora told me, reflecting on the glance she had given me in the glow of the kiosk. "Without the beard you look different. And you look heavier, fatter in the face. It makes you look more like a *barbat*."

I accepted the compliment: looking like a real man was a positive trait in Moldova. The spookiness of the space behind the buildings underlined the value of manly strength. I remembered Andrei telling me that this neighbourhood was unsafe for single people at night. Dora and I walked into the building. Inside it was black. "A couple of years ago," Dora said, "they ran out of money to light the corridors and landings." When the elevator arrived, we heard, rather than saw, its doors open. Dora pressed an invisible button whose location she had memorized. When we got out of the elevator on the seventh floor, a dim film of light enabled me to realize I had forgotten that the door of the Lencuţas' apartment looked like an iron gate in a wall. I remembered the multiple-bolted front door, but had forgotten that this door merely opened onto a mud room, beyond which lay a second double-locked, vaultlike door.

Inside the apartment was dark. I thought I knew what that meant.

Dora turned on the lights and led me into the living room. I sat down on the couch, and she took the armchair facing me. "I divorced Senya," she said. "He drank too much. Sixteen years, it ate me up. We separated two years ago, but the divorce is just going through now. That's why I didn't go to Romania this summer. He drank too much and he was turning the children against me."

She got to her feet. We moved into the kitchen where we ate sliced sausage, sliced tomatoes, and sticks of cucumber at the familiar small table. Dora made me sweet dark tea. "How old are you now?" she asked. "Are you married? Divorced?"

"Neither," I said. "I just moved back to Canada two years ago. Now I've got a steady job." I shrugged. "Who knows?"

"I got your letters," she said, referring to the Christmas cards I had sent. "I wanted to write back, but you know I can't write in Latin letters. I asked the children to write, but of course they never wanted to do anything. When I was at school, they only taught us Cyrillic. That's the only way I can write Moldovan. In the past few years I've taught myself to read the Latin letters." She seemed proud of this achievement. "But I still can't write them. I make too many mistakes."

I expressed my sorrow that her family had broken up.

"Steve," Dora said, "you have to understand that in the past few years life here has been very, very hard. Many families have broken up. It started to get really bad in 1998. All that stuff you see downtown, near your hotel—that's not for us, that's not for ordinary people. For most people things are getting worse and worse. When you're always worrying about money... And the young people leave. A lot of them go to Romania first and get citizenship. It's easier to go farther west as a Romanian than as a Moldovan. I don't know where I'll be living once the divorce goes through. Maybe I'll leave, too.

"You could go to Romania."

"I don't want to go to Romania. It's just like here—the men all drink." She thought for a moment. "I could go to Italy and work as a cleaner. A lot of people go there. They say it's the easiest language for us to learn."

It was getting late and I had to go. Dora accompanied me to the front of the development. She looked at the row of kiosks and the spread of tables in front of the Victoria Market across the street. "All these places to get drunk. How do they expect people not to drink when it's so easy?"

The next day I returned with my luggage, determined to learn more of the story.

In 1995 Andrei had married a teenage Russian girl who had been retired to Moldova by the Russian Mafia after a year working as a prostitute in Turkey. "I accepted her as she was," Dora said. "I didn't say anything about her past." Andrei and the girl set up house in the sewing room where he slept. Neither of them was working. According to Dora, they weren't even looking for work. They had a son in 1996 and a second son in 1999. "Andrei wanted the children," Dora said, "but he expected me to bring them up." The noisy, crowded apartment and constant arguments depressed Senya. His drinking, previously undertaken in secret when Dora was away, became a daily event. The more he drank, the less he worked; he began to defend Andrei's right not to work.

As in Natasha's family—in spite of all the differences—a rift occurred between the women and the men. Serge sided with male indolence by dropping out of high school at the age of fifteen. He began to steal small items from the apartment—cutlery, some of Dora's jewellery. Around this time Andrei walked out on his wife and went to live with a friend. Dora and Senya were left with the Russian girl, the two babies, and Serge, whom Dora no longer trusted. Their marriage collapsed. Dora caught Serge stealing from her and kicked him out of the apartment. "For three weeks," Dora said, "he sat out there on the bench all day in the same clothes and looked up at the apartment."

"He wanted to be forgiven," I said. I clung to my memories of Serge as an intelligent, cautious nine-year-old who had followed me to the *izvor* to fill the water bottles, raising in my chest a long lunge of paternal emotion no other child had ever inspired. How much of Dora's anger at Senya was being projected onto Serge? "Why didn't you forgive him?"

"He's no good, Seroychka. Now he lives with Andrei and steals for a living."

I couldn't suppress my shock. "But he wanted to be a lawyer—"

"You don't understand what it's like here now, Steve. You remember Borislav? He's sixteen now and he's in jail."

"But Borislav was so serious, so disciplined—"

"It's the growing up," Dora said. "Around here it's all *furt, furt, furt*—theft, theft, theft. Then they start to drink and need to pay for it. And you know that in our culture children live at home and expect to get waited on. Especially the boys. I got fed up with waiting on them all. I'm better off alone. The other day I had my girlfriends in and we sat around and talked and had such a good time. I think I'm better off alone." She looked at me, a little uncertainly, for confirmation. "A family can be good, but if it's not good, then everybody should just go his own way."

I had more questions. I asked about Valentina and Borya. Since Borislav's arrest, Dora said, they had become withdrawn. They had retreated to their *vila*, commuting in to work from the countryside. I asked what had happened to Andrei's wife and sons after he walked out. And where were Andrei and Serge living?

"Andrei has an apartment…"

"What sort of work is he doing?"

"I have no idea." I didn't believe this and expressed my disbelief with a long look. "Business," Dora said at last. "Something with his

Russian friends."

A minor Mafioso. I couldn't believe that Andrei would be very dangerous or even competent. I thought of the brawl in the café. I wondered how long Andrei would survive in that world. "And does Andrei contribute to his boys' upbringing?"

"*Foarte puţin!*" Dora said. "Hardly anything." After Andrei left, his wife had repented of her sinful past and been born again at the hands of Baptists from the United States. Dora pointed out the monstrous Baptist church that had been built opposite the Victoria Market. The red-trimmed W of its steep roof scowled out at the kiosks selling drink. Like the Victoria Market, the church held sway over Buiucani in the name of the dollar. Once Andrei's wife had converted, the U.S. missionaries had rented her an apartment in return for a pledge that the two boys would be raised in the Baptist faith. Having sold her body to the Russian Mafia, who had fielded her to the Turks, the girl had sold her sons' souls to the Americans. What else could she have done?

I returned to sleeping on the purple couch where the *ţânţars* bit my ankles. Dora, I learned, was supporting herself by taking in lodgers and sewing for a Belgian company. Western European manufacturers had discovered in neighbourhoods such as Buiucani a source of astonishingly cheap labour. Dora showed me the patterns the Belgian company had given her. She followed the patterns, took the vests and socks she produced to the warehouse the Belgians had installed in a building across the street, and received a few lei in return. Since the Belgians wished to save costs by using the same patterns for all of the former Soviet republics, the patterns were in Russian.

Dora's current lodger, Daniela, a slender young woman from a village near the Romanian border, worked in a nearby Swiss-owned textile factory. Her fifty-hour weeks earned her just enough money to rent Dora's sewing room (where Dora continued to sew during the hours when Daniela was at work). Daniela addressed Dora as "Auntie Dora." During my first hours in the apartment, the phone rang. I heard Dora ask, "When are you going to come to visit me?" When she put the receiver down, she said, "That boy lived with me for more than two years. He finished his engineering degree while he was living with me. Now he's getting married." She laughed. "He's getting married to a girl he met here. She was my lodger in the living room when he was in the sewing room. Now they've both finished at the university. When they started sleeping together, I thought, *Well, good for them!*"

She spoke of her lodgers with relish. As she described their achievements, I realized they had become her replacement children. Harbouring none of the resentments children invariably feel toward their parents, the lodgers supplied uncritical admiration. And they had succeeded where her children had failed. Daniela wasn't a university student, as the others had been, but she was a hardworking, reliable girl who made Dora proud. The only comment I could elicit from Dora concerning Andrei was: "He's become so *bad!*" When she spoke of Serge, though, her voice changed. One night she brought out every photograph she possessed of her younger son, from baby pictures to a snapshot taken a year before he dropped out of high school. She showed them to me one by one. When she finished, she said, "He's only sixteen. He's still a little boy."

While she no longer talked to Andrei or Serge, Dora continued to play a role, as Andrei had hoped she would, in bringing up her grandchildren. One afternoon I came up the stairs to find her standing in the doorway with two little boys in underpants and crew cuts. The older one, Kyril, was a cloned and shrunken version of Andrei. The younger boy, Danil, resembled Andrei less and wasn't as rambunctious. Kyril's violence was disturbing. Aged four and a half, he responded to disciplinary smacks by giving his grandmother vicious karate kicks. The boys didn't speak a word of Romanian, and Dora didn't dare impose the language on them. Her matriarchal authority shrivelled before the edifice of the Russian language. When the little boys spoke in Russian, she replied in Russian. I was struck at how everything in

Buiucani—from the signs on the Victoria Market to the Baptist church to the Belgian company's patterns to the children of the girl who had been pensioned off to Moldova by the Mafia—was flowing either toward Russian or toward English.

When the children grew unmanageable, Dora took Danil back to his mother. Returning to the apartment, she suggested we go outside with Kyril and sit *pe scaun*. I was delighted. Whenever I remembered Chişinău, I thought of the life revolving around these benches between the buildings.

In the late-afternoon light we seated ourselves on one of the two worn wooden benches that met at right angles. The grass was burned brown where it hadn't been beaten down to bare earth. The spaces between the tall, scrubby apartment blocks with their ugly crumpled balconies were cool, the sun catching only at the tops of the buildings.

The circle of women sitting on the benches kissing and smacking one another's children and grandchildren was like a little Romanian village. Kyril tore around the bare earth. When a little girl appeared with a kitten in a box, the women bent forward to offer advice on whether the animal was ill and, if it was, on how to cure it. One woman passed around a plastic bag of seeds for us to nibble. They all watched the people walking up and down the lane behind the wall of buildings: men returning home from work, groups of teenage boys hurrying along hunched together, a strolling police officer escorted by two skinny young soldiers. Against the dim thud of carpets being beaten clean on the metal frames, I saw a man walking with the step of a sailor marching on the prancing deck of an ocean-tossed ship.

"Look at him," one woman said. "Drinking."

"Look at how it destroys a man," another added.

A couple of the women glanced at Dora. "Never marry a man who drinks," a woman told her twelve-year-old daughter.

The arrival of a young woman with a baby distracted attention from the drunk. Everyone was admiring the child when a Russian woman appeared. She surveyed the benches, waited for a moment's silence, and said, "*Dobrý vecer*. Good evening."

The transformation was instantaneous. The Russian woman sat, and for the next half hour every utterance was in Russian. The mother of the twelve-year-old murmured to her daughter in Russian and the daughter replied in the same language.

When the Russian woman departed and conversation returned to Romanian, I commented on this curious phenomenon to the woman sitting next to me. Better educated than the others, she had a university degree and worked as a journalist. In most parts of the world, I said, the presence of one speaker of a different language wouldn't cause an entire group to switch languages, even among themselves.

The woman looked mystified. "But Russian is a very powerful language. It's the most powerful language in the world." She paused and took a quick look at my face. "Maybe English is becoming more powerful now, but after English, Russian is the most important language."

I tried to dissuade her of this, mentioning Mandarin Chinese, Spanish, Arabic, Hindi-Urdu. If Russian was so important, I asked, why were former Russian teachers in Poland and Hungary unemployed? Why were Russian departments shrinking and closing in universities throughout the West?

"That's not true," the woman said. "People all over the world speak Russian." It was clear nothing I said would change her mind. A half hour later a second Russian woman approached, waited for a lull in the Romanian conversation, and pronounced a hortatory: "*Dobrý vecer.*" Again, everyone switched to Russian.

I thought of my conversation earlier in the day with a Romanian-speaking politician. Having begun his career as an academic and poet, this man had moved into politics after 1991. His poetry was nationalistic, decrying the oppression of the Romanian language, though his rapt poetic craft lifted his poems somewhat above the level of sloganeering. Having bailed out of an earlier government because of his opposition to corruption (or so he told me), he appeared to be positioning himself for a future campaign for high office. He was a vigorous, articulate man in early middle age. Among Romanian-speaking Moldovan politicians, the results of the February 2001 elections had swelled the ranks of those whose titles began with the word *ex-*. Like the other ex-'s I had met, this man had a mobile telephone, no visible means of support, and bushy hair perfectly trained by a fantastically expensive haircut.

When I arrived late at a café for our first meeting, he stood next to a table for forty minutes rather than sit and risk paying for his own drink. Knowing I came from the dollar-drenched West, he emphasized three times how little money would be needed to finance a successful presidential campaign in Moldova. I barraged him with questions for an hour. At one point I said, "The percentage of Romanian speakers in Moldova is higher than the percentage of speakers of the national languages in at least two of the Baltic states. Latvia, Lithuania, and Estonia have reestablished the primacy of their national languages by bringing in strict language laws. Why can't Moldova do the same?"

That was the only moment in our conversation when this suave man looked panicked. "The Baltic states were protected by the Americans. NATO wanted a toehold in the Baltic. If we tried something similar, there would be an international scandal!" I could see him distancing himself from the more wild-eyed nationalists. "No one has a strategic interest in Moldova. NATO has bases in Turkey. They don't need to get any closer. The Russians have an interest in keeping Trans-Dniestria Russian. Aside from that, the only interest anyone has here is stability."

He met my eyes with a long, shrewd look that seemed to be assessing the impact of his words, perfecting his repertoire for the Westerners who might one day come calling with campaign funds. "If we destabilize the country, there will be a huge crisis. On the other hand, I don't think Voronin's Russification will have much effect. Certain things have changed here and there's no going back. Voronin doesn't have enough money to implement his Russification in a way that will make it effective."

I wondered about this man's sanguine approach, so at odds with the fiery poetry he had written ten years earlier. Ambition had softened his patter. As we parted, he flashed me a perfect politician's smile. "I'll send you an invitation when I'm president."

When I went to pay for our drinks, the young woman working behind the café counter took offence at my speaking to her in Romanian. Mistaking me for a local, she tried to force me to speak Russian. My friend had to intervene in Russian to calm the situation. For all its logic, I wondered whether the politician-poet's strategic explanation of Moldova's failure to reassert its language was sufficient. When Lithuania was fighting to break away from the Soviet Union, the story had ranked as front-page news in Western, particularly U.S., newspapers. Yet Moldova's plight didn't receive sympathetic airing on the front page of the *New York Times*. This was the result not only of NATO priorities, but of the existence of street-level U.S. support for Baltic autonomy. Oppressed and frustrated Baltic nationalists had fled to New York and Chicago, while oppressed Moldovan nationalists had escaped to Romania.

In part, also, the Soviet characterization of Romanian nationalism as irreducibly fascist had succeeded. Hungary had overcome its history of collaboration in the Holocaust and now enjoyed a positive image in the West; Romania and Moldova remained tarred with the brush of anti-Semitism. A couple of days earlier one of my journalist friends, barking out an approving laugh, had shown me the headline of a newspaper editorial that ran: PEOPLE WHO DON'T LIKE GENERAL ANTONESCU ARE PEOPLE WHO DON'T RESPECT OUR RIGHTS.

I wanted to scream at these men that as long as they tied their campaign for full language rights to a dead fascist general they were bound to lose. But I said nothing. It was too late. A brief opening for fuller autonomy, or reunification with Romania, had gaped before Moldovans' eyes during the tectonic shifts of the early 1990s. But that time was gone. The new millennium had carved up the planet into large, fixed blocks; globalized mass culture depoliticized populations into apathy before dominant regional cultures. Most Moldovans agreed with the woman sitting next to me on the bench that Russian was the most powerful language in the world. And, in the sense that Russian was globalization's local surrogate for the primary force of U.S.-based English-language mass entertainment culture, they were right. Cultural dominance translated into political dominance. The United States, which had embraced Russian president Vladimir Putin as a source of strategic stability, lauding his desire to "make his country strong," had underlined that rebellions against Russian over-lordship by countries such as Moldova would receive a hostile reception in the West.

Yet as I sat on the bench listening to the sounds of Russian as dusk soaked into darkness, I also felt that, at some point long before the advent of MTV, Romanian-speaking Moldovans had lost faith in themselves. They had internalized the Russian colonizers' belief in their own cultural superiority in a way that people in the Baltic states had not. Possibly the brutality of the Soviet reconquest of the country in 1944 was to blame, or possibly the explanation remained unfathomable. The result, ten years after the Soviet Union's collapse, was that while Lithuania benefitted from U.S. investment and cooperative local Russians, Moldova was saddled with U.S. Baptist missionaries and an economy directed by the Russian Mafia.

As night fell, a group of young men gathered at a picnic table half caged by a metal arbour overgrown with broad-leaved creepers. The boys were playing cards. The women—still speaking Russian—seemed to be talking about the boys. The table was too far away for me to follow the movements of the card game, though I noticed one very skinny boy with clean-cut, dusky features sitting at the end. By the time the Russian woman left and the conversation returned to Romanian, the darkness was complete. Dora suggested we return to the apartment for supper. I bid good evening to the women, and Dora, Kyril, and I walked back to the building, accompanied by a grandmotherlike neighbour of Dora's. When I mentioned that I had enjoyed sitting *pe scaun*, Dora lowered her voice. "That one at the end, she's a gossip. She remembers you from the last time you were here, but you watch, she'll be spreading it around that I have an *amant*."

We squeezed into the small, hot kitchen. The two large women stood in bare feet and long print dresses and cooked *plăcintă*, a flaky pastry pie that was an old Romanian specialty. Kyril sat at the table, watching the brown disks of *plăcintă* rise in a circular pile. "I think it's a shame Kyril doesn't speak Moldovan," the neighbour said, frowning through her glasses. "He's got a grandmother who's *moldovancă*. He's missing out by not learning the language."

"*Babushka!*" Kyril shouted. I had learned that this Russian word for *grandmother* was pronounced with a strong stress on the first syllable. Did Dora not long for grandchildren who would address her in Romanian as *bunică*?

I waited for her response, but she changed the subject. "I don't think Serge recognized Steve."

I was startled. "Serge?"

"He was playing cards," Dora said. "But without the beard and not expecting you to be here, I don't think he recognized you."

I realized Serge had been the boy at the end of the table. Stifling a longing to set out into the darkness to look for him, I saw I was going to learn only one side of this story of family breakdown. I would have to spend weeks in Chişinău in order to communicate on good terms with both Dora and her men. I suspected, though, that if Serge and Dora were still living in Buiucani in a year's time they would no longer be estranged. Each seemed to be tempting the other to end the stalemate. How long could they continue to flit past each other without speaking in the space between the buildings?

As we sat down to eat, Daniela came in from the textile factory, her light dress emphasizing her slenderness. Her long dark hair was immaculately groomed, and her face looked tired. Kyril slipped from his stool and clawed at the young woman's legs. Daniela told him to go back to the stool.

"He doesn't understand you," Dora said.

Daniela looked surprised. In her clear Moldavian Romanian, with a slight Slavic overlay in her accent, she asked, "Auntie Dora, why isn't Kyril going to the Moldovan kindergarten?" She swallowed a bite of *plăcintă*. "I don't like Russians."

"I don't have any problem with Russians," Dora said. "From 1989 to 1994 we had a lot of trouble with Russians. Now everything's calm. I don't see any problem."

Daniela didn't reply, but I could see she disagreed. Would her generation prove less accepting of its colonized status than Dora and her contemporaries had been? Or would they continue to submit, with a heightened degree of resentment?

We ate in silence until the telephone rang.

Dora stepped into the hall. We heard her shouting in Russian. The confused exchange dissolved into Romanian. "How do you expect me to recognize your voice in Russian?"

She arranged an appointment for the next day. When she returned to the kitchen, shutting the glass-panelled door behind her, she said, "That was Senya, my husband. We didn't recognize each other's voice in Russian. I didn't know who it was until he started talking in Moldovan...Romanian...whatever this language is."

The neighbour looked at her in expectation. Dora pushed herself back into our crammed-together circle. We ate the warm *plăcintă* until our stomachs were full. "I'm meeting Senya tomorrow," Dora said. "He wants this apartment, but he's not going to get it. Either I continue to live here and pay him for his share, or we sell it and divide everything in half. I think we'll probably sell it. Who knows where I'll live then? Maybe I'll be like the young people and leave the country."

Late the next afternoon, as I sat in the train travelling back to Romania, Dora and Senya met to divide the apartment.

# ACKNOWLEDGEMENTS

This book would not exist had not Elizabeth Miles perceived that it was a separate book rather than a section of a larger manuscript. I am grateful to her for that insight, and for her comments on an earlier version of the manuscript. I would like to thank Terry Byrnes for encouraging me to write about Moldova, John London for facilitating my first steps on the road to Chişinău, Ramona Fotiade for making possible my meeting with a delegation of Moldovan parliamentarians, and the Moldova scholar Charles King for taking the time to disagree with me over lunch in an Oxford pub. I am grateful to Gheorghe Pârja, Serghii Luckanýn, Nadia Moşanu, and Vlad Pohilă for helping me prepare for my return to Chişinău in 2001.

Sections of this book have been published in different form in *Matrix* and the *Montreal Gazette*.

Printed in the USA
CPSIA information can be obtained
at www.ICGtesting.com
JSHW082208140824
68134JS00014B/493

9 780888 784322